RUNNING PRESS

GEM

ANIMALS
OF THE WORLD

*A Guide to More Than
300 Mammals*

by John A. Burton
Illustrated by Bruce Pearson

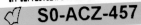

✓ **S0-ACZ-457**

Running Press
Philadelphia, Pennsylvania

First published in the United States of America in 1994 by
Running Press Book Publishers.

Text copyright © 1993, 1994 by John A. Burton.
Illustration copyright © 1993, 1994 by Bruce Pearson

Originally published by HarperCollins Publishers Limited under the
title *Collins Gem Animals of the World*

9 8 7 6 5 4 3 2 1
Digit on the right indicates the number of this printing.

ISBN: 1-56138-378-3

Library of Congress Cataloging-in-Publication Number: 93-085517

Cover design by Toby Schmidt

Printed in Italy by Amadeus S.p.A.

This book may be ordered by mail from your publisher. Please
include $2.50 for postage and handling. *But try your bookstore first!*

Running Press Book Publishers
125 South Twenty-second Street
Philadelphia, Pennsylvania 19103-4399

About this book

The purpose of this book is to provide an overview of the mammals of the world, with particular reference to those that are likely to be familiar, or those that may be seen in zoos. Most people are unlikely to be lucky enough to see more than a tiny fraction of the world's mammals in their natural state, and therefore they are most likely to see "wild" animals in the confines of a zoo or wildlife park.

Detailed descriptions have not been given when the illustration fulfills that purpose. Information is given on a wide range of topics including habitat, life-cycle, feeding behavior and breeding biology. Information on status and conservation problems is given for many species, and, since the more responsible zoos are now actively involved in captive breeding programs for rarer species, some details of the species in captivity are also given.

The animals are described by their common and their scientific names (in italics); the latter consist of two Latin words: the genus (which is capitalized) and the species. Thus, the Indian Elephant is *Elephas maxima*. When repeated, the generic name is usually abbreviated to the initial letter. Confusion can be caused by the fact that zoologists use the scientific names to indicate the relationships with other species, and occasionally the names change. Consequently, the names used in this book may differ from those used in older books.

What is a mammal?

Mammals are animals with backbones. They are also warm-blooded and covered with hair, and they suckle their young on milk. However, there are enormous variations on these basic characteristics, ranging from species that hibernate and drop their temperature to that close to the surrounding air-temperature, to species that are almost completely hairless, with only a few vestigial bristles. Other species give birth to such well-developed young that they may only suckle for a few days. Mammals are extremely diverse and have managed to colonize almost all habitats. The most adaptable of all mammals is man.

The orders of mammals

The main groups used in classifying animals are "orders" which group the main families together, and these are briefly summarized below.

MONOTREMATA – egg-laying mammals   Pages 8-9
This order comprises two families of primitive mammals which are confined to Australia and New Guinea.

MARSUPIALIA – marsupials   Pages 10-19
There are over 280 species of marsupial. They are found in South America and Australasia, with a single species in North America.

XENARTHRA – toothless mammals   Pages 20-25
There are 29 species of toothless mammal – anteaters, armadillos and sloths.

INSECTIVORA – insectivores   Pages 26-35
There are about 365 species of insectivore, generally rather small mammals, with small teeth, which typically feed on invertebrates. They are found in most parts of the world except Australasia.

SCANDENTIA – tree shrews   Pages 36-37
There are 16 species of tree shrew found in S.E. Asia. They are sometimes classified with the insectivores or, more often, with the primates.

DERMOPTERA – flying lemurs   Pages 38-39
This order comprises the two species of flying lemur.

CHIROPTERA – bats Pages 40-47
Nearly 1,000 species of bat have been described so far, and new species are likely to be discovered, particularly in the tropical forests.

PRIMATES – primates Pages 48-75
There are over 200 species of primate, including the lemurs, bushbabies, marmosets, monkeys, apes and man. They are found on all continents.

CARNIVORA – carnivores Pages 76-115
The approximately 235 species range in size from the tiny weasel to the polar bear and tiger.

PINNIPEDIA – seals Pages 116-123
There are approximately 35 species of seal, sealion and the walrus. They are sometimes classified with the Carnivores.

CETACEA – whales and dolphins Pages 124-131
The 77 species of cetacean comprise two main groups: the toothed whales (dolphins, sperm whales and porpoises) and the baleen whales.

SIRENIA – sea cows Pages 132-133
There are four living species of sea cow, all found in warmer, tropical waters.

PROBOSCIDEA – elephants Pages 134-137
There are two living species of elephant.

PERRISODACTYLA – odd-toed ungulates Pages 138-149
There are 16 species of odd-toed ungulate (hoofed

mammal), including horses, rhinos and tapirs.

HYRACOIDEA – hyraxes   Pages 150-151
There are 8 species of hyrax in Africa and Arabia.

TUBULIDENTATA – aardvark   Pages 152-153
This order consists of a single species, the aardvark of
Africa.

ARTIODACTYLA – even-toed ungulates   Pages 154-199
There are nearly 200 species of even-toed ungulate or
hoofed mammal, including pigs, peccaries, deer, camels, antelope, sheep, cattle and their relatives.

PHOLIDOTA – scaly ant-eaters   Pages 200-201
There are 7 species of pangolin or scaly ant-eater in
Africa and Asia.

RODENTIA – rodents   Pages 202-221
This order is made up of approximately 1,800 species,
mostly small mammals, distributed almost worldwide.

LAGOMORPHA – rabbits   Pages 222-225
There are about 65 species of rabbit, hare and pika,
found mostly in the northern hemisphere, but also
south in Africa, and introduced elsewhere.

MACROSCELIDEA – elephant shrews   Pages 226-227
There are about 15 species of elephant shrew, all confined to Africa. They are sometimes classified with the
insectivores.

ECHIDNAS

The **Short-nosed Echidna** or **Spiny Anteater** *Tachyglossus aculeatus* is found in Australia, Tasmania and south-eastern New Guinea. It grows to nearly 2 ft. long and weighs up to 13 lbs.; it does not have a tail or external ears. The much rarer **Long-beaked Echidna** *Zaglossus brunijni* occurs in New Guinea. Unlike the Short-nosed Echidna the hair on its back often nearly hides the spines, and the underside usually lacks spines. Echidnas are egg-laying mammals (monotremes), usually laying one egg into a pouch.

Short-nosed Echidna

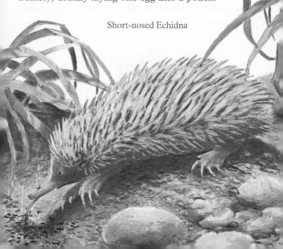

DUCK-BILLED PLATYPUS
Ornithorhynchus anatinus

The **Duck-billed Platypus** is an egg-laying mammal, the only other monotreme, related to echidnas. The female does not have nipples, but exudes milk through pores in her skin. It is found in freshwaters of Australia and Tasmania. It is very aquatic and covered in soft, thick fur. The feet are webbed and the tail flattened and beaver-like in appearance. As its name suggests, the bill is duck-like and rather rubbery and it uses this as it searches river beds for food, including insects, worms, tadpoles, and other aquatic life. It is also one of the few venomous mammals, the males having spurs with poison glands.

BRUSH-TAILED POSSUM
Trichosurus vulpecula

There are 3 closely related brush-tailed possums native to Australia. The Brush-tailed Possum is the species most commonly seen in zoos and is found wherever there is suitable habitat throughout Australia, Tasmania and Kangaroo Island, but is absent from some of the more northern areas. It has been introduced into New Zealand, where is has become an abundant pest.

THE BUSHY-TAILED OPOSSUM
Glironia venusta

Although most marsupials are confined to Australia, the opossums are found in Central and South America, with a single species, the **Virginia Opossum** *Didelphis virginiana*, occurring north in the United States, as far as New England. The **Bushy-tailed Opossum** is one of the rarest opossums known, and is little-studied. Fawn or cinnamon brown above, it is paler below and has a dark facial mask. It grows to a body length of about 8 in., and as its name suggests, has a long, bushy tail of about 9in. It is thought to feed on insects and berries. Only five specimens have ever been found and four of these came from commercial animal dealers. All the specimens were from humid tropical forests in the Upper Amazon regions of Ecuador, Peru and Bolivia. Although so little is known about this animal (and virtually nothing is known of its biology), it could prove to be more widespread and abundant than current data suggests. However, its survival will largely depend on its tropical forest habitat not being destroyed.

GREY KANGAROOS

There are two closely related species of grey kangaroo, or Forester: the **Eastern Grey Kangaroo** *Macropus giganteus* and the **Western Grey** (or **Sooty** or **Black-faced**) **Kangaroo** *M. fuliginosus.* The Western is found in open woodland in southern and southwestern Australia, while the eastern is found in similar habitats in eastern Australia and Tasmania. Grey kangaroos are among the largest marsupials, with a body length of 4½ ft., a tail of 3 ft. and a weight of up to 200 lbs. They live in small parties, grazing on grasses, herbs and other vegetation usually at twilight or at night. The single young (or joey) weighs about 1 oz. at birth and is finally

Eastern Grey Kangaroo

weaned at about 14 months. It overlaps with the next young in the pouch, for shortly after a joey is born another is conceived, though its development after birth is delayed until the previous young has left the pouch. The huge hind feet enable kangaroos to make enormous leaps, and males also fight with them. Like the Red Kangaroo, the Grey is persecuted by farmers and is also exploited for its meat and hide. The Eastern Grey Kangaroo is exhibited in many zoos where it breeds quite regularly and may live for 15 years or more. The Western Grey Kangaroo is more rarely seen. When moving slowly they have a "five-footed" gait, balancing on their tails and forelegs, while swinging the hind legs forward.

TREE KANGAROOS

Bennett's Tree Kangaroo
D. bennettianus

There are about 7 species of tree kangaroo – although some of the species may have been described twice, since they are rather variable and occur over quite a large area, mainly in mountainous rain forests in New Guinea and northeastern Queensland, Australia. Most species are occasionally seen in zoos, but among the most frequently seen are the **Ornate** or **Goodfel-**

low's **Tree Kangaroo** *Dendrolagus goodfellowi* (illustrated on this page), the **Grizzled Tree Kangaroo** *D. inustus* and **Matschie's Tree Kangaroo**, *D. matshiei*. They are fairly large, ranging in size between 1 ft. 8 in. and 2 ft. 7 in. long, plus a tail of up to 3 ft., and weigh up to about 20 lbs. Some are strikingly marked. Matschie's Tree Kangaroo is one of the most brightly colored of all marsupials. Unlike the terrestrial kangaroos, their limbs are more or less equal in proportion. They have large feet, and pads on their soles which help when climbing. Although the thickly furred tail is not prehensile, it aids balance. Tree Kangaroos are very agile, they can make leaps of up to 30 ft. from tree to tree and jump to the ground from heights of 60 ft. without hurting themselves. They feed mostly on fruit and leaves. After a gestation of about 32 days, a single young is born. They are slow growing, first emerging from the pouch at about 10 months and continue to suckle until nearly 14 months. Matschie's Tree Kangaroo has lived up to 14 years in captivity. The rarest species are the **Unicolored Tree Kangaroo** *D. dorianus*, which is now being bred in a few zoos, and Goodfellow's Tree Kangaroo which is bred in some numbers. Both are from New Guinea.

COMMON WOMBAT *Vombatus ursinus*

The **Common Wombat** was once found over most coastal regions of Australia, from south-east Queensland to south-east Australia and Tasmania. They look like small bears, growing up to 4 ft long and a weight of up to 77 lbs. They occur mainly in forests in rocky habitats where they dig a complicated network of burrows. The closely related **Hairy-nosed Wombat** *Lasiorhinus latifrons* is considerably bigger, with a hairy nose and larger, more pointed ears.

Common Wombat

KOALA BEAR Phascalarctos cinereus

The **Koala Bear** has a
"teddy bear" appearance
with very soft fur
for which it was
once on the verge
of extinction; over
2 million skins were
being exported in
1924 alone. Fortu-
nately, due to protec-
tion since then, num-
bers have recovered and
it is now found through-
out most of its former
range. Confined to eucalyp-
tus forests, they feed almost
exclusively on the leaves and
bark of these trees, as well as on
mistletoes and American box *Tristania*.
The single young (occasionally twins) stays in the
mother's pouch for 7 months and is then carried on
her back. Koala Bears are particularly difficult to breed
in captivity and are seldom seen outside Australia.

SUGAR GLIDER *Petaurus breviceps*

The **Sugar Glider** or **Flying Phalanger** is the marsupial equivalent of a flying squirrel, growing to a total length of about 14 in. of which the bushy tail is over half. Like flying squirrels, it is not capable of true flight, but makes extended leaps of up to 165 ft. by means of the gliding membrane which stretches along the flanks between the fore and hind feet. Widely distributed around Australia, except in the west, they have also been introduced into Tasmania. Mainly arboreal, they rarely descend to the ground, and feed at night on nectar, blossoms, buds and insects. The **Squirrel Glider** *P. norfolkensis* is related to the Sugar Glider, but larger with a more distinct stripe on its back; it is found in eastern Australia.

EASTERN QUOLL OR NATIVE CAT
Dasyurus viverrinus

The **Eastern Quoll** was a common species in S. E. Australia until the 1930s, even around Adelaide and Melbourne, but since then it has become very rare and may even be extinct on mainland Australia. However, populations still survive in Tasmania, although these, too, are threatened by an epidemic disease which has been present since the turn of the century. Its coloring is rather variable, ranging from greyish olive-brown to brown or black, with buff or white spots on the back and sides. A carnivorous marsupial, it feeds on a wide variety of small animals, including rats, mice, and insects, as well as on some plants, and occasionally raids poultry.

The **Giant Anteater** *Myrmecophaga tridactyla* (above) was once found in open forest and savanna in South America from northern Argentina to Guatemala and Belize. Due to human disturbance and hunting, it is now rare or even extinct over much of its former range. It grows to about 4 ft., plus a tail of 3 ft. and weighs up to 86 lbs. It feeds on termites and ants, ripping open the mounds with powerful claws and gathering ants, larvae and eggs with a long sticky tongue, eating up to 30,000 in one day. Anteaters also occasionally eat other insects. The remarkable tongue can be extended over

2 ft., but measures about ½ in. across at its widest part. A single young is born after a gestation of about 190 days and is carried on the mother's back. A Giant Anteater has lived over 25 years in captivity.

There are two species of **Tamanduas** or **Lesser Anteaters**: *Tamandua tetradactyla*, which is found in South America east of the Andes from Venezuela to Uruguay, and *T. mexicana*, found from southern Mexico to Peru and Venezuela. They grow up to 2 ft. 6 in. plus a tail of just over 2 ft. and weigh up to 15 lbs 6 oz. Tamanduas live in more forested areas than the Giant Anteater, and spend much of their life in trees where they are excellent climbers using their prehensile tails. They feed on ants and termites. Although popular zoo exhibits, Tamanduas are rarely bred in captivity. The **Silky** or **Dwarf Anteater** *Cylopes didactylus* is a rarity in zoos. It is found in forests from Mexico to Bolivia and Brazil, rarely, if ever descending to the ground.

Tamandua *Tamandua tetradactyla*

SLOTHS

Two-toed Sloth *C. hoffmanni*

Three-toed Sloth *B. tridactylus*

There are about 5 species of sloth (depending on their classification), all confined to Central and South America. They are exclusively tree dwelling and find it difficult to walk on the ground. However, several extinct species of ground sloths are known, and some may still have been in existence when the first Europeans visited the New World. The largest of these were as big as elephants. The surviving sloths are adapted to living upside down in trees, and their camouflage is enhanced by growths of algae on their fur.

There are 2 closely-related species of **Two-toed Sloth:** *Choloepus hoffmanni* found from Nicaragua, south to Ecuador, and *C. didactylus* found east of the Andes to the Amazon basin. They grow to a maximum of 2 ft. 6 in., lack a tail, and weigh up to 19 lbs. A particular peculiarity of the Two-toed Sloth is that, whereas most mammals consistently have 7 neck vertebrae, Two-toed Sloths have 6, 7 or 8. A single young is born after a gestation of up to 11.5 months (or much shorter). They breed freely in captivity and have lived over 31 years in zoos.

The 3 species of Three-toed Sloths have similar habits to the Two-toed: the **Pale-throated Sloth** *Bradypus tridactylus* is found in southern Venezuela, the Guiana and northern Brazil; the **Brown-throated Sloth** *B. variegatus* from Honduras to northern Argentina and the Maned Sloth *B. torquatus,* the rarest, is found in the rapidly disappearing coastal forests of south-eastern Brazil. The habitat of all is threatened.

ARMADILLOS

There are about 20 species of armadillo known, all found in the Americas. Most are found in fairly open country, but the largest, the **Giant Armadillo** *Priodontes maximus* (up to 130 lbs.), is mainly forest dwelling. The smallest is the Fairy Armadillo *Chlamyphorus truncatus* and the most widespread the **Nine-banded Armadillo** *Dasypus novemcintus* (above), found from Uruguay northwards throughout Central America, into the USA. Since the beginning of this century, the Nine-banded Armadillo has considerably expanded its range in the USA, partly due to deliberate introductions, and it continues to spread. It grows to about 2½ ft. and weighs up to 14 lbs., but normally 9 lbs.

The litter nearly always contains 4 young, born after a gestation of 4 months. A peculiar feature of their reproduction is that all the young in any particular litter come from a single fertilized egg, and are consequently identical quads of the same sex. The life spans of armadillos are poorly known, but in the wild, Nine-banded Armadillos are believed to live up to 7 years.

The Three-banded Armadillo *Tolypeutes matacus* is found in Bolivia, Brazil, Paraguay and Argentina in open areas. Like the previous species it feeds largely on insects such as ants and termites. It normally give birth to only a single young after a gestation of 120 days. The newborn young are miniatures of the adults, although the eyes and ears are not open, they are able to walk and roll up into a ball.

Although armadillos are exhibited in many zoos and have been bred in laboratories, they are only rarely bred in zoos. In the wild, they are preyed upon by many carnivores, but the biggest threat to this species comes from cars which cause many deaths. Their skins have also been used extensively in the curio trade for the manufacture of folk guitars and other souvenirs and their meat has also been important.

Three-banded Armadillo defensive posture

TENRECS

There are about 30 different tenrecs, all of which are confined to Madagascar. Tenrecs are small insectivores which have filled most of the ecological niches occupied by shrews, hedgehogs, moles and other small insectivores found in other parts of the world. There are aquatic species such as the rare **Web-footed**

Tenrec *Limnogale mergulus,* and burrowing, mole-like species such as the **Rice Tenrec** *Oryzorictes talpoides.* The rarest is the forest-dwelling *Dasogale fontoynonti* which is only known from a single specimen. One of the commonest species is the rabbit-sized **Tail-less Tenrec** *Tenrec ecaudatus* which grows to about 14 in. and a weight of 7 lbs. It is very prolific and litters of 12 are common, and up to 21 have been recorded. Like all tenrecs, it feeds on insects and other invertebrates and any small mammals it encounters. The **Greater Hedgehog-tenrec** *Setifer setosus* is only about one-third the size of a European Hedgehog, but is equally spiny and rolls into a ball when in danger. It is occasionally exhibited in zoos. The **Lesser Hedgehog** or **Pygmy Tenrec** *Echinops telfairi* is also sometimes seen in zoos.

Rural peoples sometimes hunted tenrecs for food

HEDGEHOGS

The **Northern Hedgehog** *Erinaceus europaeus* grows to about 10 in. long (its tail is small and concealed) and weighs around 1¾lbs., increasing to 3 lbs. before hibernating. It is widespread and often common over most of north-western Europe, and in New Zealand, where it has been deliberately introduced. Two other similar species also occur in parts of Europe; the **Algerian** or **Vagrant Hedgehog** *E. algirus*, which is found in south-west Europe and North Africa, and the **Eastern Hedgehog** *E. concolor* of eastern Europe. Hedgehogs are mainly nocturnal and are found in a wide variety of habitats; the European Hedgehog has adapted to many man-made ones. They feed on a variety of invertebrates and other

European Hedgehog

small animals, birds' eggs and reptiles (including poisonous snakes). The Northern Hedgehog has 2-9 young in a litter, born almost naked and with soft spines after a gestation of 30-48 days. A second litter is occasionally produced, but the young from this are less likely to survive the winter hibernation. Hedgehogs are often kept in zoos but are only rarely bred, and it is unlikely that there are any self-supporting captive populations. They have lived for 6 years or more in captivity, but are much shorter lived in the wild.

Several other species of hedgehog are sometimes exhibited in zoos, including the **Long-eared Hedgehog** *Hemiechinus auritus* which is found from eastern North Africa through Arabia to India and Mongolia. The Moonrats of south-east Asia are related to hedgehogs but, although similar in many ways, lack the hard spines of true hedgehogs. The largest known insectivore is the Moonrat *Echinosorex gymnurus*.

Long-eared Hedgehog

SHREWS

Pygmy and **Common Shrews** are red-toothed shrews, a group of shrews which is widespread in the northern hemisphere. Both species are widespread, being found from Britain and France eastwards to Siberia. The Pygmy Shrew *Sorex minutus* measures about 2 in. plus a tail of up to 2½ in. The Common Shrew *S. araneus* is medium sized, growing to 3 in., plus a relatively short tail of about 2 in. Very similar species also occur in North America.

Water shrews, which also have red-tipped teeth, are found throughout most of Europe (except Iberia, south-east Europe and most islands), including Great

Common Shrew

Southern Water Shrew

Britain. They are relatively large, growing to a total length of up to 6 in. of which the tail is less than half. There are two species, similar in appearance, but the **Southern Water Shrew** *Neomys anomalus* is white below. Both swim and dive well.

There are several species of white-toothed shrew in Europe (and new species still being discovered). They are found in a wide variety of fairly dry but well vegetated habitats and it can be difficult to distinguish the different species. They are widespread in southern central and eastern Europe but only the **Lesser White-toothed Shrew** is found in Britain and then only in the Isles of Scilly. The **Pygmy White-toothed Shrew** is the smallest known mammal, weighing less than 0.1 oz. and measuring up to 2 in. in length plus a tail of up to 1¾ in. The **Bicolored** is distinguished by its pale underside and contrasting darker upperparts, but all these shrews are difficult to identify and may be confused with the red-toothed shrews unless the teeth are examined.

Bicolored with young

MOLES

European Mole

There are 11 very closely related and very similar species of mole in Europe and Asia. The **European Mole** *Talpa europeae* is found in most of Europe except the Mediterranean, occurring as far north as Britain and southern Sweden. It is found mainly in wooded habitats and meadows wherever there is soil for burrowing, and will also move into rural gardens where it is usually exterminated because of its burrowing activities. They spend most of their life tunnelling underground using the enlarged fore-paws to dig. In addition to their powerful fore-paws, moles have several other adaptations to their subterranean life. Their eyes are reduced, or in some species actually covered with skin, and their fur is short and velvety and can be brushed in any direction, enabling them to move backwards with ease.

Their tunnels are often clearly visible, as are the molehills which are pushed up at intervals. However, in forests where moles can also be abundant, these runs are usually hidden by leaves. In very dry weather, moles may often be seen above ground.

The young are born naked and helpless in an underground nest which is lined with grasses. Their diet consists mainly of earthworms and some species are known to store surplus worms by disabling them with a bite. In North America, related species occur, including the **Star-nosed Mole** *Condylura cristata*, which has 22 fleshy tentacles on its nose.

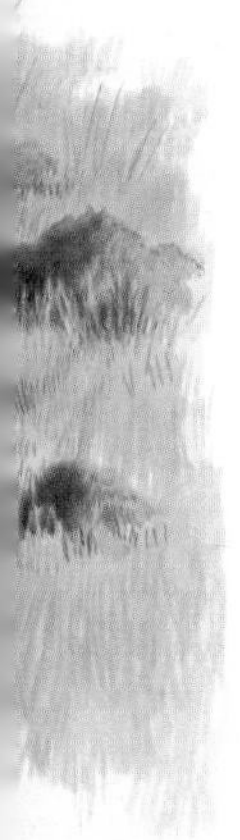

molehills

DESMANS

The desman is a web-footed member of the mole family of which two species survive – the **Pyrenean Desman** *Galemys pyrenaica* (above) and the **Russian Desman** *Desmana moschata*. The former grows up to 5 in., with a very long tail of up to 6 in., while the latter is much larger, growing up to 18 in. in total length. They are among the most aquatic of mammals, living in cold, fast-flowing rivers; their spatulate snout can be used as a snorkel, and they have water repellent guard hairs which protect the dense insulating underfur. They are rarely seen as they are nocturnal.

GOLDEN MOLES

There are about 18 species of African Golden Mole, only occurring in central and southern Africa, some of which are widespread and abundant and others with very restricted ranges. They are rather similar to true moles, but the brownish fur usually has a metallic lustre or iridescence. They have no tail, the eyes are vestigial and covered by skin, and the nostrils are protected by a flap of skin. Some Golden Moles feign death (like opossums) when dug up. One of the rarest (illustrated), **Gunning's Golden Mole** *Amblysomus gunningi*, is only known from a small area in East Transvaal, South Africa. Originally thought only to occur in Woodbush Forest, in 1974 it was discovered in the Agatha Forest Reserve 12 miles away.

COMMON TREE SHREW *Tupaia glis*

Tree shrews are among the largest of the insectivores and are of considerable interest to zoologists as they are often considered to be closely related to the ancestors of monkeys, apes and man, which probably looked similar to tree shrews. Although they are also related to shrews, in some ways they behave more like squirrels and their scientific name comes from the Malay *tupai*, which is used for any squirrel-like animal. All 16 of the tree shrews are found in India and south-east Asia. The **Common Tree Shrew** is the most widespread species, found from the Himalayas eastwards to southern China and south to the Malay Peninsula, Sumatra, Borneo and Java. It grows to 8 in., plus a bushy tail of 7 in., and weighs up to 6 oz. Common Tree Shrews are mostly diurnal and live mainly in thick undergrowth and low bushes, where they are agile climbers. They are omnivorous, feeding not only on insects, including ants and termites, but also on a variety of fruits and other plant matter which they hold in their front paws – their thumbs and first toes are opposable, enabling them to grip. They are also fond of water, drinking at and bathing in the pools found in tree hollows. They defend territories against intruders of their own kind, often noisily. They build nests in tree holes or under logs and breed at all times of the year, with 1-3 young born after a gestation of up to 56 days. The young leave the nest when just over 1 month old. In some areas, Common Tree Shrews are abundant and have adapted to man-made environments, even entering houses. They are the only kind of tree shrew normally seen in zoos but, although they are often exhibited, only a few zoos are breeding them successfully. Like many insectivores, tree shrews are comparatively short-lived in the wild, although they can live for 2 or more years in captivity.

Malayan Colugo
Cynocephalus variegatus

FLYING LEMURS

The two species of colugo or flying lemur belong to a distinct family, but zoologists are still uncertain as to their closest relatives. Although they are not capable of true flight, they may be related to bats, or to insectivores – they are *not* related to the lemurs. One species, *Cynocephalus volans* is confined to the islands of the southern Philippines, the other, the **Malayan Flying Lemur** *Cynocephalus variegatus,* is more widespread, found from southern Thailand and Indochina, south through the Malay Penisular to Sumatra, Borneo, Java and many other islands. They are totally arboreal and use the huge membranes which stretch between the neck, the fore and hind limbs and the tail to glide for 330 ft. or more. Although they cannot fly, their gliding abilities are remarkable and one was measured to lose less than 40 ft. of elevation in a glide of 450 ft. between two trees. Colugos feed on fruit, flowers, shoots and buds. They are believed to live in small groups and normally give birth to a single young, which is very underdeveloped and carried in a fold of the mother's gliding membrane which forms a marsupial-like pouch.

FRUIT BATS

There are about 170 species of Fruit Bat or Flying Fox, the largest of the bats. One of the largest of these is the **Indian Flying Fox** or **Greater Indian Fruit Bat** *Pteropus giganteus* which has a wingspan of over 4 ft. It is found from India eastwards to western China and south to Sri Lanka and the Maldive Islands. Indian Flying Foxes spend the day in noisy roosts in the tops of trees, and may even roost in the centre of cities such as New Delhi. At dusk they leave the roost in search of fruit, which they chew to extract juice and then they spit out the pulp. They fly with characteristic slow wing-beats and may travel considerable distances to feed. In some fruit-growing areas, they are regarded as a pest. Although the Indian Flying Fox is not endangered, most of its close relatives have very restricted ranges and several are endangered; some may already be extinct. The **Egyptian Fruit Bat** *Rousettus aegyptiacus* is one of the smaller fruit bats, with a head and body length of only 5 in. It is widespread in many parts of Africa, through the Middle East (including Cyprus and Turkey) to Pakistan. In some parts of the world, notably the Pacific and Indian Ocean islands, Fruit Bats are considered a delicacy to eat and in these places this may have been instrumental in their decline. However, a much more serious threat to overall populations is loss of forest habitat. They are also hunted for sport. The fruit bats adapt to captivity better than most smaller bats, and some of the rarer species are being bred in captivity.

BATS

In addition to the fruit bats, there are 17 other families of bats comprising over 800 species. These occur in almost all parts of the world, in almost all habitats, even managing to migrate to arctic forests and mountain tops. However, they are most diverse and numerous in tropical forests. Many species roost in caves and some of the greatest concentrations of a mammal species known are those of cave roosting bats, with several millions congregating in a single cave system. Most bats navigate by echo-location, emitting high-frequency sound and using the echos for avoiding objects (sonar). Bats are generally long-lived – 20 or more years is not an uncommon life expectancy even for the smaller species – and have rather slow reproductive rates. Some species migrate for several hundred miles. Most bats are insectivorous, but some have adapted to feeding on nectar (and several are important pollinators of trees and plants in tropical forests), and a few have evolved to become carnivorous. The most specialist of all is the Vampire Bat, which feeds exclusively on the blood of mammals and birds. Insectivorous bats are generally difficult to keep in captivity, although some zoos have developed nocturnal exhibitions where they have been shown successfully, and they rarely breed in captivity.

LONG-EARED BATS

Grey Long-eared Bat

The six closely related species of long-eared bat occur in both the Old and New World. They are relatively small, with a head and body length of up to 3 in., and easily recognised by their huge ears which can be over 1½ in. long. The **Grey Long-eared Bat** *Plecotus austriacus* occurs in Europe, as far north as southern England where it is very rare, south to North Africa and Senegal, and east to Mongolia and China. The **Common Long-eared Bat** *Plecotus auritus* is more widespread in northern Europe, and one of the most abundant bats in Britain. It is a medium-sized bat with a body length of up to about 2 in., and enormous ears which are nearly as long as the body; when at rest the ears are folded under the wings. They can often be seen flying among trees, hovering and picking insects and spiders off leaves. It also occurs widely across Europe and Asia to Japan. Very similar species occur in North America such as **Townsend's Big-eared Bat** *Plecotus townsendi* which is endangered over most of its range. Long-eared bats often roost in houses, mines and other man-made structures, and while this may have helped them to increase their range, they are also vulnerable to disturbance and to poisoning from insecticides used in timber treatment. The long-eared bats all hibernate for at least part of the winter, and the females usually gather in nursery colonies during the breeding season. In some species, these colonies can number 1,000 females.

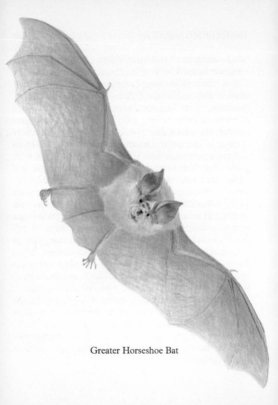

Greater Horseshoe Bat

HORSESHOE BATS

There are about 70 species of horseshoe bat found exclusively in the Old World. Their range extends from Europe (except the north), throughout most of Africa, east throughout most of Asia to Japan and south to Australia. The **Greater Horseshoe Bat** *Rhinolophus ferrumequinum* is one of the best known and most widespread species, occurring from southern Britain to Morocco and east to Japan. It has declined dramatically in recent years and the populations in Britain and most of northwestern Europe are now less than 2% of their numbers at the turn of the century, and are considered endangered. Many other species of horseshoe bat are also thought to be drastically reduced in number, but in most cases little is known of their status. The most distinctive feature of the horseshoe bat is the complex nose-leaf structure, which is used in projecting the high-pitched sound used in echo-location. When roosting they hang free, with their wings wrapped around their bodies. Most species are colonial, often roosting in dense clusters. In the northern parts of their range they hibernate, and it is in these hibernating roosts that they are particularly vulnerable. Disturbance which wakes them up uses up valuable fat reserves and may cause them to die if it occurs too frequently.

LEMURS

Ring-tailed Lemur

Black Lemur
Lemur macaco

male   female

The Lemurs are confined to Madagascar (with a single species in the Comoros, probably introduced). There are 4 families: Cheirogalidae (mouse lemurs), Indriidae (known as leaping lemurs or indri and sifakas), Daubentonidae (the Aye-aye) and Lemuridae (the remaining 16 species of lemurs). The **Ringtailed Lemur** *Lemur catta* belongs to the latter family and occurs in forested areas of southern Madagascar. It grows to a length of up to 18 in. plus a tail of up to 20 in., and is less arboreal than most other lemur species. When walking on all four feet it holds its tail erect. The **Aye-aye** *Daubentonia madagascariensis* is the only living member of its family and is found in bamboo and mangrove forests where they are arboreal and nocturnal. Destruction of forest habitat has led to their decline and they are now reduced to scattered individuals. The **Indri** *Indri indri* has thick silky fur and its song is audible to humans for up to 1½ miles. Although rare, they occur in a few reserves in Madagascar.

Indri

GALAGOS

Greater Galago

There are about 7 species of bushbaby or galago, all African, but only 2 are common in zoos: the **Greater** or **Thick-tailed Galago**, *Otolemur crassicaudatus* and the **Senegal Bushbaby** or **Lesser Galago** *Galago senegalensis*. The Greater Galago grows to about 18 in., plus a tail of 20 in., and weighs up to 4 lbs. It is found south of the equator to the Tropic of

Capricorn. The Senegal Bushbaby is under half the size of the Greater Galago, growing to 8 in. plus a tail of 1 ft., and weighing 11 oz. It is widespread over much of Africa south of the Sahara, except for the extreme south and the Zaire River Basin. The smallest species, **Demidoff's Galago** *G. demidovi*, weighs about 3 oz. It is rarely seen in zoos. Three other species are also very occasionally seen – **Allen's Galago** *G. alleni*, the **Western Needle-clawed Galago** *Euoticus egantulus,* and *O. garnetti,* a close relative of the Greater Galago.

Bushbabies are agile climbers and are often sociable. As their large eyes suggest, they are strictly nocturnal. They feed on a wide variety of plants and insects, and also on lizards, birds and other small animals. Up to 3 young are born after a gestation of nearly 150 days. Both the Greater Galago and the Senegal Bushbaby are frequently bred in zoos, where they have lived for up to 14 years.

Demidoff's Galago

TARSIERS

There are 3 species of tarsier which have a sparse distribution in south-east Asia. They have spectacularly large eyes, soft pale olive, reddish or greyish fur and a long tail which only has fur at the end. The fingers and toes are slender, ending with pads and pointed nails, except on the second and third toes of the hind feed which have large claws. They are arboreal and nocturnal, feeding exclusively on small animals including insects, lizards and amphibians. All species of tarsier are extremely rare, threatened not only by loss of habitat but also suffering from the effects of pesticides in plantations. The **Western** or **Horsfield's Tarsier** *Tarsius bancanus* grows to a body length of up to 6 in. and its tail can be up to 9 in. long. They have been known to occur in large groups in densities of up to 300 per sq. mile, but are now thought to be endangered and are protected in Sarawak, Sabah and Indonesia. The **Eastern** or **Sulawesi Tarsier** *T. spectrum*, is confined to three areas on Sulawesi and a few adjacent islands. Although it has legal protection in Indonesia, little is known of its status. The **Philippine Tarsier** *T. syrichta*, is declining throughout most of its range due to the destruction of its forest habitat and it is not known to occur in any protected areas.

Philippine Tarsier

Sulawesi or
Eastern Tarsier

Western or
Horsfield's Tarsier

DOUROUCOULI

The **Douroucouli, Night Monkey** or **Owl Monkey** *Aotus trivirgatus* is an almost entirely nocturnal species found in Central and South America, from Panama south to Paraguay. They live at altitudes of up to 6800 ft (2100 m)and are found in a wide variety of forest habitats where they build daytime nests of twigs and leaves in hollows, clefts or among vines. Douroucoulis grow up to 15 in. long, plus a tail of up to 16 in., and they weigh about 2 lbs. Their large owl-like eyes give them excellent nocturnal vision, and they are very agile, leaping from branch to branch. Unlike many other South American monkeys, the Douroucouli's tail is not prehensile. They feed on fruit, nuts, berries, flowers, insects and other small animals. Douroucoulis live in small groups, usually consisting of a pair of adults and their young. They are very vocal – over 50 sounds are known, including a call lasting several seconds and resonated with a throat sac. A single young is born after a gestation of about 150 days, and is mature at about 2 years. Douroucoulis used to be popular as pets, and they are exhibited in many zoos, particularly those with a nocturnal house. They breed regularly, and have been bred through several generations; in captivity, they have lived for over 13 years.

By contrast, three species of titi monkey *Callicebus* spp., which superficially resemble Douroucouli, although diurnal, are comparatively rare in zoos. The **Masked Titi** *C. personatus* is the rarest species in the wild, and none are known to be in zoos at the time of writing. The **Dusky Titi** *C. moloch* can be seen in a few zoos and is occasionally bred in captivity.

SQUIRREL MONKEYS

There are 2 very closely related species of Squirrel Monkey: the **Common Squirrel Monkey** *Saimiri sciureus,* which is widespread in South America from Colombia to Paraguay, and the **Red-backed Squirrel Monkey** *S. oerstedi,* which is confined to Costa Rica and Panama. The Common Squirrel Monkey grows to a

Common Squirrel Monkeys

length of 14 in. plus a tail of 17 in., and weighs about 2 lb. Apart from the marmosets and tamarins, they are the smallest primates in South America. Squirrel Monkeys live in troops of up to 300 or more, in a wide variety of mainly forested habitats where they feed on fruit, seeds and other plant matter, as well as on insects and other small animals such as frogs and snails. They are the most gregarious of all South American primates and within the troops they divide into subgroups, and an extremely large number of sounds are made as they encounter one another. After a gestation of 152-172 days a single young is born, which is carried about clinging to the mother. They become independent after 1 year; females mature at 3 years, males at 5, and in captivity they have lived for over 12 years. Squirrel Monkeys have long been popular, not only in zoos but also as household pets and dressed in dolls clothes as street photographers accessories – they were favourites with organ grinders. During the 1960s and 1970s, tens of thousands were involved in trade and large numbers were also used in bio-medical experiments. The Red-backed Squirrel Monkey is endangered by loss of habitat, and until recently was also being exploited for the pet trade. Spraying against yellow fever and malaria may also have harmed Squirrel Monkeys and other wildlife. There are a few small colonies of Red-backed Squirrel Monkeys in captivity, and the Common Squirrel Monkey is one of the most common primates in zoos.

BLACK-HANDED SPIDER MONKEY

The **Black-handed** or **Geoffroy's Spider Monkey** is found from southern Mexico, south through Central America to north-western Colombia. They are long-limbed with a long prehensile tail, growing to a length of 17 in., plus a tail of over 20 in. and weighing up to 11 lbs. They are nearly as agile as the gibbons of Asia, and can swing through the trees using their tail as an extra limb, but normally run along the top of branches with their tails arched over their backs. They live in comparatively large troops in a wide variety of forest habitats, including mangroves, where they are largely opportunistic feeders, eating a wide range of fruits, nuts and other plant matter, and also eggs, insects and other small animals. In the wild they are known to attack intruders by breaking off branches weighing 10 lbs. or more, and hurling them down. The single young is born after a gestation of about 230 days, and females become sexually mature at 4 years, males at 5 years. In captivity, one spider monkey has lived for 33 years. There are 3 other species of spider monkey: the **Long-haired Spider Monkey** *Ateles belzebuth*, the **Brown-headed Spider Monkey** *A. fusciceps* and the **Black Spider Monkey** *A. paniscus*, all from northern South America. All are threatened, and several populations are extremely rare, or even extinct. In addition to forest destruction, they are collected for trade and have also been extensively hunted as human food. The Black-headed Spider Monkey is commonly seen in zoos, the others more rarely.

MARMOSETS

There are about 17 species of marmoset and tamarin, all found in Central and South America, and mostly in the Amazon region. They are the smallest primates, and the smallest of all is the **Pygmy Marmoset** *Cebuella pygmaea*, which grows to a length of 6 in., plus a tail of up to 9 in., and weighs under 5 oz. Twins are usual, born after a gestation of about 20 weeks, and they mature at about 1½-2 years. Unlike many other Marmosets, the Pygmy does not appear to be endangered as it is well able to adapt to man-made and disturbed habitats after the forest has been cleared.

The **Lion Tamarin** *Leontopithecus rosalia* is one of the world's rarest animals, and all 3 subspecies, the **Golden Lion Tamarin** *L. rosalia rosalia*, the **Golden-headed Lion Tamarin** *L.r. chrysomelas* and the **Golden-**

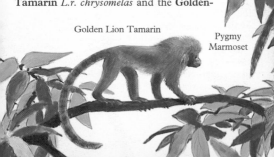

Golden Lion Tamarin

Pygmy Marmoset

rumped **Lion Tamarin** *L.r. chrysopygus*, are endangered, with possibly less than 300 altogether in the wild. The Lion Tamarin grows to about 1 ft., plus a tail of up to 16 in., and weighs up to about 25 oz. The long silky "mane" gives it its name. They live in small family groups and 1-3 young (usually twins) are born after a gestation of up to 132 days. The largest and most widespread of the marmosets are the **Long-tusked Marmosets** or **Tamarins** *Saguinus* spp. There are about 11 species, one or more of which are found in most parts of Central and South America. The White-lipped Tamarin *S. labiatus* is found in central Amazonian Brazil and the **Red-handed Tamarin** *S. midas* in northern Brazil and the Guianas.

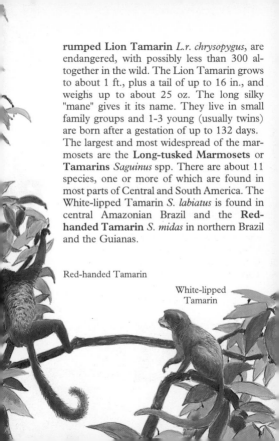

Red-handed Tamarin

White-lipped
Tamarin

MACAQUES

The macaques are among the hardiest and most widespread of all the monkeys. There are about 13 species found in North Africa (and Gibraltar), southern and eastern Asia north to Japan, and south to the islands of South-east Asia. Most macaques are gregarious, living in troops numbering half a dozen to 100 or more. The **Rhesus Macaque** *Macaca mulatta*, which occurs from eastern Afghanistan through northern and central India to Burma and south-eastern China, is one of the best known of all primates, being used in hundreds and thousands for the preparation of polio vaccine and other medical and scientific experiments. Although in the wild it is the most abundant of the macaques, and is probably increasing in urban areas, it is thought to be declining rapidly in many rural parts of its range.

Black Ape

Toque Macaque

The **Celebes Macaque** or **Black Ape** *Macaca nigra* is the most distinctive of all the macaques, and is confined to the Celebes and neighbouring Butung in South-east Asia. Unlike most other monkeys, it is often carnivorous, hunting other animals such as birds, lizards, and rodents in addition to the macaque's more usual diet of berries, fruits and nuts.

The Toque Macaque *M. sinica* is another species confined to an island – Sri Lanka. It is closely related and similar in appearance to the Bonnet Macaque *M. radiata* of southern India. The Toque is the smallest macaque, with a total length of about 3 ft., of which the tail is half.

The **Japanese Macaque** *M. fuscata* is the most northerly of monkeys. Some live high in the Japanese alps on a diet of seeds and bark in a habitat covered in snow for much of the year.

Japanese Macaque

BABOONS

The **Olive** or **Anubis Baboon** *Papio anubis* grows to about 3 ft., plus a tail of up to 2½ ft., and weighs up to 66 lbs.; females are smaller than males. It is found in Africa from the River Niger eastwards to Kenya and is closely related to several other species.

The **Guinea Baboon** *P. papio* is found in eastern Senegambia north to Mali and Mauritania; the **Yellow Baboon** *P. cynocephalus* occurs from Somalia to Mozambique and Angola; the **Chacma Baboon** *P. ursinus* is found in South Africa, as far north as Zambia, and the **Hamadryas Baboon**

Olive Baboons

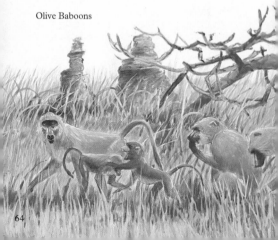

P. hamadryas in north-east Africa and south-west Arabia. All are rather similar, except the Hamadryas male which has a very well-developed mane and whiskers. Baboons live in troops, led by a dominant male, which may number 100 or more. Usually a single young is born after a gestation of up to about 190 days; it is weaned at 8 months and sexually mature after 4 years. Baboons are omnivorous and mostly live in open country, often near rocky ravines, and wander extensively. Many populations have been exterminated, particularly in northern parts of Africa. The Olive and Hamadryas Baboons are most commonly seen in zoos, where they often live for 30 years or more.

SAVANNAH MONKEYS

South African
Vervet *C. aethiops
pygerythrus*

Tantalus
Monkey
*C. aethiops
tantalus*

Green Monkey
C. aethiops sabae

Grivet
*C. aethiops
aethiops*

The **Savannah Monkey** (also known as the **Vervet, Grivet, Tantalus Monkey** and **Green Monkey**, depending on the subspecies) grows to a maximum of 3 ft., plus a tail of about 4 ft. and weighs up to 5½lbs.; females are smaller than males. Very variable in color and pattern, some 21 subspecies have been described. Savannah Monkeys are often found close to human habitation in open country throughout most of Africa south of the Sahara, up to altitudes of 13,000 ft. They may be abundant in agricultural lands, where they can be serious pests, but are absent from rainforests and drier habitats. They feed on a variety of plants, small animals, and cultivated crops, and are prey for the larger cats, eagles, pythons, crocodiles and even baboons. They may live in troops of 100 or more, but usually in smaller family parties led by an old male. In common with several other of the Cercopthecine monkeys, the male has a spectacular threat display exposing his erect red penis and blue or white scrotum in front of his white belly fur. After a gestation period of up to 200 days, a single young (occasionally twins) is born which is clasped to the mother until about 10 days old when it can hang on by itself. The young start to explore at 3 weeks, are suckled for 6 months and mature at about 2½ years. Savannah Monkeys have been exploited for biomedical research and for the pet and zoo trade. Large numbers were also killed for their fur. They have lived for 24 years in captivity and are exhibited in most large zoos where they breed regularly

COLOBUS

Black Colobus

Angolan Black-and-white Colob

Gueraza

Red Colobus *Colobus badius*

Olive Colobus *Procolobus verus*

The male **Black-and-white Colobus** *Colobus poly-komos* grows to just over 2 ft., plus a tail of up to 3 ft. and a weight of 44 lbs.; females are slightly smaller. The proportions of black and white fur vary enormously over their range, which extends through the forests of west and central Africa to Angola and Kenya. They are strictly arboreal, living and feeding mainly in the forest canopy. They make enormous leaps and to escape danger they plunge down to the lower levels of the forest using the springiness of the branches to catapult themselves to safety. They live in small family groups led by a male, feeding mainly on leaves, together with bark, seeds and insects. They breed all year round and the single white young is born after a gestation of up to 178 days. The baby begins to explore and jump at 3 weeks, but still returns to the mother when in danger until about 1 year old. Females are mature at 2 years, males at 4. They have lived up to 20 years in captivity, but relatively few zoos have been really successful in keeping colobus, and only a handful breed them.

The similar **Gueraza** *C. guereza* and **Angolan Co-lobus** *C. angolensis* are occasionally seen in zoos, but the various reddish brown species of colobus *C. badius*, *C. kirki* and the **Black Colobus** *C. satanus* are rarely seen. Colobus fur has been (and still is) used for coats, trimmings and the regalia of African chiefs, and this, added to the loss of forest habitat, threatens or endangers many populations.

LANGURS

Dusky or Spectacled
Langur (male)

Langurs are rather slender-bodied, up to 2½ ft. in length, with a long tail, sometimes over 3 ft., and long hands. They are mostly greyish above and paler below, and in some species the sexes have different coloring, and the young are more brightly colored. Of the 15 species, 10 give cause for conservation concern, but they are probably all declining in some parts of their range. Diurnal forest dwellers, they are generally arboreal, feeding almost entirely on vegetable matter, including leaves, flowers and fruits; they also raid crops. Among the most threatened is the **Dusky** or **Spectacled Langur** *Presbytis obscura* which, although still locally

female

common in Thailand and possibly Burma, has declined sharply in Malaysia, due to continuing deforestation. The **Common Langur** or **Hanuman** *P. entellus* is the most common and widespread langur, found throughout most of India and eastern Sri Lanka. However, despite being protected in India and considered sacred over most of its range, because it can cause serious damage to agriculture it is persecuted and hunted in some areas.

COMMON GIBBON *Hylobates lar*

The **Common Gibbon** (also known as the **Lar, White-handed, Dark-handed, Silvery,** and **Grey Gibbon,** depending on the subspecies) once occurred throughout the forests of south-east Asia. Now, with the disappearance of much of its forest habitat, its range is fragmented into isolated pockets. Living in small family groups they proclaim their presence at daybreak with a chorus of calls. They "brachiate", or swing from arm to arm, through the trees and can cover 10 ft. in a single swing, and leap over 30 ft.

GORILLA *Gorilla gorilla*

The largest of the apes, male **Gorillas,** grow to a height (when standing) of up to 6 ft., and weigh up to 440 llbs.; females are usually much smaller. Gorillas live in troops of up to 30 or more animals of a wide range of ages, led by a dominant male. They feed almost entirely on vegetable matter, particularly leaves and shoots, fruits and tubers. The **Mountain Gorilla,** thought to number fewer than 400, is found in rainforest with dense undergrowth in eastern Zaire, Rwanda, and Uganda. In Rwanda a conservation program which allows tourist visits to the Gorillas has proved successful and numbers appear to be increasing. However, they are still threatened by loss of forest habitat and hunting.

Lowland Gorilla
adult male

Mountain Gorilla
adult male

CHIMPANZEES

The **Chimpanzee** *Pan troglodytes* grows to a standing height of up to 5½ ft. and a weight of 120 lbs.; females are smaller. Chimpanzees are social animals sometimes living in troops of 60 or more, feeding on a variety of plant and animal life. Formerly found in a wide variety of forest and more open habitats throughout West Africa south of the Sahara as far east as western Tanzania and south to the Zaire river, the Chimpanzee's range has now become very much reduced and fragmented. South of the Zaire River, the closely related **Pygmy Chimpanzee** or **Bonobo** *P. paniscus* is found. Smaller and more lightly built than the Chimpanzee, they are little-studied in the wild, and do not occur in any major protected areas. Both species are considered endangered.

Chimpanzee

Pygmy Chimpanzee

ORANG-UTAN *Pongo pygmaeus*

Heavily built, an adult male **Orang-utan** can weigh as much as 220 lbs. Their name means "man of the forest" and in their forest habitat males are usually solitary, while females are accompanied by their young. They keep mainly to the trees and brachiate (swing from arm to arm), each swing covering over 6 ft. They feed mostly on fruit and other vegetable matter, but occasionally take small animals. Endangered in the wild and now confined to small areas of Sumatra and Borneo, there are large numbers in captivity, including several successful breeding colonies.

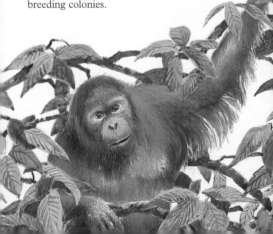

WOLF *Canis lupus*

The **Wolf** is similar in appearance to jackals and German shepherd dogs, growing to about 5½ ft., including a tail of up to 18 in. Variable in appearance, animals in the north are heavily built and thickly furred, whereas in desert areas they tend to be rather small and rangy. Once widespread throughout the northern hemisphere, including the British Isles, it is now extinct or endangered over most of its range.

ARCTIC FOX *Alopex lagopus*

Arctic Foxes occur widely all around the polar regions in both the Old and New Worlds from Alaska to Siberia, as well as on most northern islands. Despite the enormous numbers that are trapped for their fur, they are still widespread and abundant and do not appear to be endangered. They are fairly small, growing to a total length of about 3 ft. of which the tail is about one-third, standing about 1 ft. at the shoulder and weighing up to 20 lbs. There are 2 distinct color phases, which may occur side by side: in one, the summer coat is brownish and turns white in winter; in the other phase, it is brownish-grey in summer and smoky bluish-grey in winter.

Adult, winter

RED FOX *Vulpes vulpes*

The **Red Fox** is, throughout its range, one of the most abundant larger predators. It is widespread throughout the northern hemisphere as far south as the southern states of the USA, and in North Africa as far south as the Nile Valley; it has also been introduced into Australia. The **North American Fox** is sometimes regarded as a separate species, *Vulpes fulva*, and there are several other closely related species which are similar to the Red Fox. These include the **Cape Fox** *V. chama* from South Africa, the **Pale Fox** *V. pallida* and the **Sand Fox** *V. rueppelli* both from around the Sahara; and the **Bengal Fox** *V. bengalensis* from India. The Red Fox grows to a total length of up to 4 ft., of which the tail is about one-third, and may weigh up to 22 lbs. It normally breeds in underground dens and has 3-8 (max. 13) cubs after a gestation of up to 56 days. It is an opportunistic feeder, taking a wide variety of animals including mice, earthworms, ground-birds, and frogs, but particularly voles. It also scavenges. Red Foxes have adapted to man-made environments and are often found in suburban and urban areas. They have been bred in captivity extensively, particularly in North America where a variety of color variations such as silver fox and cross-fox have been especially bred for the fur industry.

SPECTACLED BEAR *Tremarctos ornatus*

The **Spectacled Bear** grows up to 6 ft. long and weighs up to 385 lbs., but usually less. It is uniform black, or dark brown, except around the eyes and on the neck. This is the only bear found in South America, where it once occurred from Panama as far south as Brazil and Argentina. Now restricted to mountainous regions of western South America, it is mainly nocturnal, hiding in hollow trees or rocky clefts by day. Their diet consists mostly of fruit and other vegetable matter, they are particularly partial to palm hearts and cacti fruit (even climbing large cacti to reach them). They will also eat insects, rodents, and other small animals. One of the world's rarest bears, they have been hunted for meat and as a trophy, and because of their depredations on crops. However, populations in more remote parts of their range are probably reasonably safe.

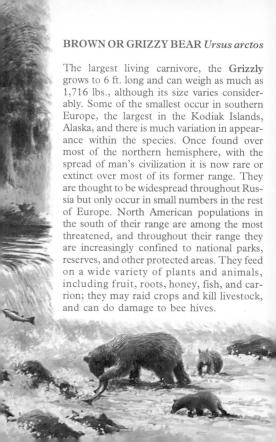

BROWN OR GRIZZY BEAR *Ursus arctos*

The largest living carnivore, the **Grizzly** grows to 6 ft. long and can weigh as much as 1,716 lbs., although its size varies considerably. Some of the smallest occur in southern Europe, the largest in the Kodiak Islands, Alaska, and there is much variation in appearance within the species. Once found over most of the northern hemisphere, with the spread of man's civilization it is now rare or extinct over most of its former range. They are thought to be widespread throughout Russia but only occur in small numbers in the rest of Europe. North American populations in the south of their range are among the most threatened, and throughout their range they are increasingly confined to national parks, reserves, and other protected areas. They feed on a wide variety of plants and animals, including fruit, roots, honey, fish, and carrion; they may raid crops and kill livestock, and can do damage to bee hives.

POLAR BEAR *Thalarctos maritimus*

Polar Bears are found around the North Pole, in arctic Canada, Alaska, Russia, Scandinavia, and Greenland. They are almost marine in many parts of their range, living on ice floes and never coming to actual land. Unlike most other bears, they do not have territories but wander continuously, even on floating icebergs. Although Polar Bears have been kept in menageries, circuses, and zoos for many years, only in the last few decades have they been bred successfully in captivity. In Tudor times, a Polar Bear kept in the Tower of London was allowed to catch fish in the Thames. At one time on the verge of extinction, after many years of strict protection they are now considered to be out of danger, and are once more hunted in small numbers by Inuits. They are almost entirely carnivorous, feeding mainly on carrion, fish, seals, and birds, but in summer take some lichens, mosses, and berries. Females spend the winter in a den excavated in the snow where 1 or 2 cubs are born after a gestation of about 240 days. Tiny at birth, weighing about 1 lb., the cubs do not leave the den until about 4 months old, and do not become independent until their second year. Young Polar Bears are very playful, often gambolling in and around the water with their mothers. When fully grown they are one of the largest of the bears, up to 8 ft. long, about 4½ ft. at the shoulder and weighing up to 990 lbs. They have lived up to 33 years in captivity.

RACCOON *Procyon lotor*

Originally found only in North America, where it is widespread and often quite common, the **Raccoon** is now found living in the wild parts of Europe, including the Baltic republics and Russia as a result of escapes from fur farms. The Raccoon grows to a length of about 3 ft., of which the tail is approximately one-third, and weighs up to 33 lbs. Raccoons are very active, intelligent, and very dexterous, using their forepaws as hands. Their German name of *Waschbär*, and French name of *Raton laveur*, as well as the Latin *lotor*, all derive from their habit of washing their food. They are omnivores, but mainly eat animals, after hunting along rivers and streams where they find crustaceans, fish, molluscs, and amphibians, as well as insects, birds, and their eggs and small mammals. They also eat fruit and other plant matter and carrion. They make a den in a hollow tree, a rock cleft or even in another animal's burrow, and the cubs (usually a litter of 4) are born in spring. The cubs may remain with the mother until the following spring, but usually disperse in the autumn. Although Raccoons may lie up in their dens during the winter, they do not actually hibernate. Raccoons are popular exhibits in zoos where they breed freely. They have also been captive-bred on a large scale by commercial fur farms. They have lived for 14 years in captivity. Raccoons often live close to man, scavenging in dustbins, and in many parts of North America they are often seen as road casualties.

There are another 6 closely related species of raccoon found in Central and South America; 5 of them are found only on islands and are little known and some may even be extinct. The sixth, the **Crab-eating Raccoon** *P. cancrivorus* is found from Costa Rica south to Peru and Uruguay.

GIANT PANDA
Ailuropoda melanoleuca

The **Giant Panda** has a very restricted distribution and is only found in a handful of remote mountainous bamboo forests in China. Its diet consists almost entirely of bamboo, although its bear-like teeth show that its ancestors were carnivores, and pandas may still eat small animals when they find them. At long intervals, the bamboos flower and then die off, and it is thought that this may be one of the causes of the panda's rarity. In 1975-6, after the bamboo died, nearly 150 pandas were found dead, and no doubt many more died without being found. The Giant Panda has been adopted as the symbol of the World Wildlife Fund and has come to symbolize rare and endangered species, just as the Dodo symbolizes total extinction. In 1937 Chicago Zoo was the first to exhibit a Giant Panda (Su Lin), and, ever since, pandas have remained the most popular (and valuable) of all zoo animals. By 1980, over 30 had been exhibited outside China, living for up to 14 years in captivity. In the 1970s, several were presented by the Chinese Government to major zoos throughout the world. They have been bred in captivity in China for several years, and recently other zoos have been successful. The Giant Panda is one of the best-known and most distinctive of mammals. It is generally bear-like in appearance and grows to nearly 6½ ft. and a weight of up to 265 lbs. It gives birth in winter to 2 tiny helpless young of which only one normally survives. Pandas do not become sexually mature until about 6 years old.

STOAT & WEASEL

Stoats and **Weasels** and their close relatives are among the smallest carnivores. One or more of them are found in nearly all parts of the world except for Australia (they have been introduced into New Zealand). For their size, they are voracious predators, often tackling animals considerably larger than themselves. Both the Stoat *Musela erminea* and the Weasel *M. nivalis* are widespread in Europe, parts of Asia and North America. In the more northerly parts of their range, both species turn white in winter, the Stoat retaining the black tip to its tail. This black tip is characteristic of ermine, used for trimming regalia and seen in heraldry. Weasels and Stoats are often persecuted for their alleged predation of game-birds, and they are also often hunted for their pelts, which are used in their hundreds of thousands in the international fur trade. They feed on a wide variety of rodents, ground-birds, rabbits and other animals. Stoats have 1 litter per year of 5-6 kittens born after a gestation of about 2-12 months. Weasels have 2 litters of up to 10 kittens born after a gestation of only 35 days. Fully grown Stoats measure 16 in., of which the tail is about one-quarter. Weasels grow to only 8 in., plus a tail of 2 in., females are even smaller. Male Stoats weigh up to 10½ lbs., Weasels up to 4½ lbs. Several species of Weasel have been bred successfully in captivity and have been studied by biologists in laboratories.

Stoat

Stoat in winter (Ermine) Stoat molting

Weasel

89

BADGERS

The **Eurasian Badger** *Meles meles* (above) is widely distributed over most of Europe, across Asia to Japan. Although it has now disappeared from much of its former range, it is still surprisingly abundant in some areas.

Badgers are mostly nocturnal and live in extensive burrows known as setts. Two or 3 young are born in early spring after a gestation of about 65 days. They emerge from the sett at 6 weeks old, grow to 3 ft. long and are mature at 2 years. They have lived for 16 years in captivity. The **American Badger** *Taxidea taxus* is similar in appearance to the Eurasian Badger, and is widespread in North America from California and central Mexico north to central Canada. It is mainly nocturnal and in the wild is most likely to be seen along highways at dusk or dawn. It digs extensive burrows and also digs in search of rodents, which are its main prey. Two to 5 young are born in early spring, and when fully grown are about 2½ ft. long and weigh up to 22 lbs. Although they eat large numbers of rodents, American Badgers are often persecuted because of their burrowing; in the past, they have also been hunted for their pelts. They are rarely seen in zoos outside North America, but they have lived for up to 12 years in captivity.

American Badger

Domesticated Mink

MINK

Mink are among the best known and most valuable fur bearing animals, and the **Wild American Mink** *Mustela vison* is still extensively trapped for the fur trade; this species is the ancestor of the mink kept on fur farms. In the wild, it is found in or near rivers and lakes throughout Canada and much of the USA. It has also escaped from fur farms, or been deliberately introduced, in Britain and other parts of Europe, where it is often considered a pest. The European Mink *M. lutreola* is endangered in western and northern Europe, but occurs in scattered populations in eastern Europe through to Siberia. Both species grow to about 2 ft., of which the tail is just under one-third. They are mainly found in aquatic habitats, are good swimmers, and feed on a wide variety of small animals including frogs, voles, water-birds, and fish.

European Mink

American Mink

POLECATS

Polecats are small carnivores closely related to the domestic ferret. The **European Polecat** *Mustela putorius* grows to about 2 ft. of which the tail is about one third, and weighs between 1-3 lbs. Both the Steppe Polecat *M. eversmanni* and the **Marbled Polecat** *Vormela peregusna* are slightly smaller. Female polecats are smaller than males. Polecats are found in a wide range of habitats, usually fairly wooded, often near human habitations. The Steppe Polecat is found mainly in open country. The rarest ferret in the world is the **Black-footed Ferret** *M. nigripes* which is almost indistinguishable from the Steppe Polecat, but lives in Prairie-dog cities on the borders of Canada and the USA, and was thought to be extinct until a few were rediscovered in 1981. These have been bred in captivity and small populations released into the wild.

Steppe Polecat

STRIPED SKUNK *Mephitis mephitis*

One of the best known mammals in North America, the **Striped Skunk** is famous for its ability to spray an evil-smelling fluid from an anal gland over a distance of 15-20 ft. This is used to deter predators, for in addition to its foul smell, it temporarily blinds the intruder. It is found from Canada, through the USA to northern Mexico. It grows to over 2½ ft. including a tail of up to 16 in., and weighs up to 4½ lbs.; males are larger than females. It is mainly nocturnal and is omnivorous, feeding on a wide variety of animals and plants including mice, insects, berries, fruit, and carrion. It makes its den in burrows, hollow logs, rock piles, and under buildings, where the females bear up to 10 young (usually 5 or 6) after a gestation of up to 63 days. In the northern parts of its range, the skunk sleeps for days on end in cold weather, but does not go into true hibernation. When they leave the nest, the young follow the mother in single file. Although large numbers of skunks are killed on roads, and were once hunted for their skins, they are still abundant over most of their range. The Striped Skunk is the species most commonly seen in zoos, where it is occasionally bred and has lived for 13 years. There are a number of related species, including the **Hooded Skunk** *M.macroura*, 4 species of spotted skunks *Spilogale* spp, and 7 species of hog-nosed skunks *Conepatus* spp. All are confined to the New World.

EURASIAN OTTER *Lutra lutra*

The **Eurasian Otter** was once widespread throughout Europe, North Africa and Asia as far south as Java and Sumatra. In most of western Europe, however, except for Scotland, Ireland and parts of Scandinavia, and some other parts of their range, otters are now extinct or very rare. They live in rivers, lakes, estuaries and sea coasts, and eat a wide variety of fish, particularly eels, as well as rodents, frogs, birds, crustaceans and even carrion. The Eurasian Otter grows to about 4 ft. 3 in. including the tail, which is about one-third of the total length, and weighs up to about 33 lbs. The closely related **American River Otter** *L. canadensis* is almost identical in appearance and behaviour and is widespread in the Americas. It is often exhibited in zoos.

Up to 5 cubs (usually 2 or 3) are born at any time of the year after a gestation of about 60 days in a burrow (holt), usually close to water. The cubs are blind at birth and open their eyes at about 4 weeks; they leave the nest at about 6 weeks and are independent at 6-9 months. Otters are very playful, even when adult, making slides on river banks and tobogganing in snow. Although they are often kept in zoos, the Eurasian Otter rarely breeds in captivity. However, experimental reintroduction programmes of captive-bred and hand-reared otters have been started. The Otter Trust in England has specialized in breeding European Otters.

LINSANG

The **African Linsang** *Poiana richardsoni* is found in separated areas in West and Central Africa – from Sierra Leone to Zaire, and also on the island of Fernando Po. They are confined to rain forests where they are entirely nocturnal and generally arboreal and feed on a variety of small animals including insects, birds, and lizards, and also on fruit. They build nests in which to sleep, and give birth to 2 or 3 young. The African Linsang is genet-like in appearance, but with a proportionally longer tail, growing to a length of up to 1 ft. 3 in. plus a tail of up to 16 in., and weighing up to 1 lb. 9 oz.

Spotted Linsang

There are two other species of linsang, both found in Asia: the **Banded Linsang** *Prionodon linsang*, found from Thailand south to Java and Borneo, and the Spotted Linsang *Prionodon pardicolor* which is widespread from Nepal, eastwards to Indo-China. The latter is very similar in size and appearance to the African Linsang. The Banded Linsang is so called because the markings on the back join together to form broad bands. In habit they are very similar to the African species. Because they are all found primarily in mature forest, it is likely that their range is decreasing. Although they adapt readily to captivity, they are not often seen in zoos, and only rarely breed in captivity. A Banded Linsang has lived for over 8 years in captivity.

Banded Linsang

EGYPTIAN MONGOOSE
Herpestes ichneumon

The **Egyptian Mongoose** or **Ichneumon** is
widespread in Africa and occurs in a great variety of habitats, except for the deserts of
the Sahara and south-west Africa. It is also

found in southern Europe. This species, together with several other of the 15 *Herpestes* mongooses, is sometimes seen in zoos. The best known is probably the **Indian Grey Mongoose** *H.edwardsi*, immortalized as Riki-Tiki-Tavi by Rudyard Kipling, and to be seen captive in many street snake-and-mongoose fights in India and the Far East. Mongooses are mainly active by day and sleep in a burrow, hollow log, or rock crevice. They feed on a wide variety of rodents, birds and their eggs, reptiles, amphibians and crustaceans, and are able to kill poisonous snakes because they move fast and have the added protection of a coarse fur around the neck which deflects bites. After a gestation of 49-77 days, up to 4 (usually 3) young are born. Both parents help to rear the young. When fully grown, at 1 year, they are around 3 ft. long, of which the tail is about one third, and weigh up to 9 lbs. They are sexually mature at 2 years old.

HYENAS

Brown Hyena

Striped Hyena

Spotted Hyena

The 3 species of hyena are closely related to the Aardwolf. The **Brown Hyena** *Hyaena brunnea* grows to a length of up to 4 ft., a height of 2½ ft. and weight of 120 lbs. It is the rarest and least widely distributed, restricted to southern Africa south of a line approximately from south Angola to the Zambesi in Mozambique. The **Striped Hyena** *H. hyaena* grows to a length of up to 4 ft., a height of 2½ ft. and weighs 100 lbs.; the male is slightly larger than the female. It was once widespread over the northern half of Africa, through Asia Minor, the Middle East and southern Asia to India. The **Spotted Hyena** *Crocuta crocuta* grows to a length of up to 6 ft., a height of 3 ft. and weighs up to 190 lbs.; females are the larger. It is widespread in most of the more open habitats in Africa south of the Sahara. Once thought to be scavengers, hyenas are now known to be powerful predators whose kills lions often scavenge. They take a wide variety of animal prey, as well as carrion and fruit, and even raid badly buried human remains. They crush and eat bones, which makes their droppings a characteristic chalky-white. Spotted and Striped Hyenas are the species most frequently seen in zoos, where both breed occasionally. The Striped Hyena is usually solitary, except during the breeding season when it lives in pairs and the male helps to rear the 2-4 young. The Spotted Hyena lives in pairs or small groups, and occasionally in troops of 100 or more. Striped Hyenas have lived for up to 24 years in captivity, and Spotted Hyenas for up to 40 years.

European
Lynx

Bobcat

Caracal

104

LYNX, BOBCAT AND CARACAL

Between them, these medium-sized, closely related, short-tailed cats are (or were) found over most of North America, Europe, Asia and Africa. The **Lynx** *Felis lynx*, the most northerly species, found mainly in well-wooded habitats in Europe, Asia, the northern USA, and Canada, and once widespread in the woodlands of Europe, is now reduced to isolated populations. One of these, the more heavily spotted **Pardel Lynx**, found in south-west Spain and Portugal, is endangered. The **Bobcat** *F. rufus* is found from southern Canada through the USA to Mexico, and the **Caracal** *F. caracal* over most of Africa, Asia Minor, Arabia, southern Russia, and east to central India. The Lynx grows to about 4 ft. 3 in. plus a tail of 10 in., the Bobcat to about 2 ft. 6 in. plus a tail of 9 in. and the Caracal to 3 ft., plus a tail of 1 ft. They all feed on a wide variety of birds and mammals, and the Caracal has even been trained in India and Iran to hunt hares and game-birds. A litter of 2-3 kittens is born after a gestation of 50-60 days. They mature at about 1 year and may breed the following year. Lynx and Bobcat are exploited for the fur trade, particularly in Canada and the USA where they are extinct in many parts of their ranges. In captivity, Lynx have lived for up to 18 years, Caracals for 17 years, and Bobcats for 25 years. Captive-bred Lynx have been successfully re-introduced into Sweden and other parts of Europe, and with protection are slowly recolonizing some areas.

PUMA *Felis concolor*

The **Puma, Mountain Lion** or **Cougar** was formerly found almost the length and breadth of the Americas, but has been persecuted relentlessly as it is regarded as a threat to livestock. Pumas are extinct or rare over most of their North American range and considerably reduced in numbers throughout Central and South America, particularly where they are close to human settlements. Nearly as large as the Jaguar they can grow to 9 ft., including a tail of 3 ft., and frequently weigh up to 220lbs. However, they vary greatly in size and coloration, the smallest animals occuring in the tropics. Outside the breeding season, pumas are usually solitary. Found mainly in mountainous areas, they will take virtually any prey, from insects to horses, but their preferred prey is deer.

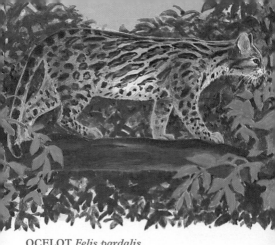

OCELOT *Felis pardalis*

The **Ocelot** has a wide distribution throughout South and Central America and as far north as Texas. However, it is becoming increasingly rare, many populations are endangered, and it is extinct in many areas. It has been relentlessly hunted and trapped for the fur trade and large numbers of young Ocelots were once imported into the USA as pets. Found in a wide range of habitats, including arid semi-deserts and tropical rainforests, it is also suffering from loss of habitat. Generally nocturnal and arboreal, it feeds on small birds, rodents, reptiles and other animals up to the size of small deer.

LION *Panthera leo*

Male **Lions** grow to about 6½ ft., plus a tail of 3 ft., and weigh up to 440lbs.; they are markedly bigger than females and normally have impressive manes. The Lion was once found throughout the more open parts of Africa and south-east Europe, and east through Asia Minor and Arabia to India. It is now extinct in the northern part of its range, except for an isolated population in the forest of Gir in India. It survived in the Middle East until well into this century. They are often vocal, and the male's roar can be heard by humans up to 5 miles away. Lions generally hunt by day or night, usually in groups (prides), preying on a wide variety of large mammals and also scavenging. They hunt by stalking their prey, and by making a final charge, suffocating or strangling large prey and killing small animals with a swipe from their paw. After a gestation of up to 113 days a litter of up to 4 (usually 2-3) cubs is born in a den in a thicket among rocks. The cubs are spotted at birth. They are weaned at 6 months, but are not sexually mature until 18 months and not fully grown until 5 or 6 years. Lions breed prolifically in captivity, where they have lived for up to 30 years, and there is a considerable annual surplus of captive-bred animals.

Asiatic Lion

Siberian Tiger

TIGER *Panthera tigris*

The **Tiger** is the largest of the cats, growing to a maximum of about 10 ft. of which the tail is just over one third. There is, however, enormous variation in size – those from Siberia being the largest and those from

Indonesia the smallest. Tigers once ranged from Asia Minor and the Middle East, across Siberia and India to Korea and Manchuria in the east, and south to Bali, Sumatra and Java. Now, remnant populations are confined to India, Siberia, and south through Indo-China to the Malay achipelago. Their numbers are also a fraction of former times. The decline is largely due to persecution, particularly in the colonial period, when thousands were killed annually until the 1950s. Tigers are usually solitary and, due to persecution, nocturnal. After a gestation of 105-113 days up to 6 (usually 1-4) kittens are born. They are weaned at about 11 weeks and are sexually mature in their fourth year. Tigers are one of the most popular exhibits in zoos and they breed freely – some females have produced over 30 cubs. They have lived for 26 years in captivity.

Bengal Tiger

JAGUAR *Panthera onca*

The largest cat in the New World, the **Jaguar** grows to 9 ft., plus a tail of 2 ft. 6 in., and can weigh over 220 lbs. Its color is variable but generally tawny with black spots which form rosettes. Completely black Jaguars also commonly occur. Once found in the southern USA and throughout most of Central and South America, due to habitat destruction and hunting they have been exterminated over a large part of their range and are now considered threatened. They are excellent climbers and swimmers and feed on a variety of mainly mammal prey, including peccaries, deer, tapir, capybara, and on large birds, small caimans and freshwater turtles.

LEOPARD *Panthera pardus*

The **Leopard** was once widespread over almost the entire continent of Africa, and also throughout southern Asia from Turkey to eastern China and south to the Malay archipelago and Sri Lanka. They have been extensively hunted and used in the fur trade and are now rare or extinct in many parts of their range. Markings are variable, typically consisting of rosettes, but black "panthers" also occur.

CHEETAH *Acinonyx jubatus*

The **Cheetah** is a large, long-legged cat with a short, rather small head. It grows to a length of up to 4½ ft. 7 in. plus a tail of 2½ ft., and weighs up to 132 lbs.; females are slightly smaller than males. Cheetahs were formerly widespread and occurred in most of the more open habitats in Africa, and also north and east through the Middle East to India. Now they are only found in a small area in Iran and Turkmenistan and in Africa south of the Sahara, where they are mostly declining or very rare. They hunt by day and feed mainly on mammals, which they run down at speeds of up to 69 mph (110 kph) – they are the fastest land mammals. They usually knock their prey over, then seize it by the throat and strangle it. Most hunts are unsuccessful, and consequently disturbance by humans can have a very harmful effect by reducing their success rate even further. Their preferred prey is usually gazelles, such as impalas, and the calves of larger antelope. Cheetahs live singly, in pairs or in small family groups, but usually hunt alone. After a gestation of about 95 days up to 6 (usually 2-4) kittens are born, which are weaned by 3-6 months and independent at about 18 months. Cheetahs are fairly vocal; they purr in contentment, and also have a loud yelp that can be heard by humans 1½ miles away. In the past, Cheetahs were frequently tamed and kept for hunting gazelles and antelope in India and other parts of Asia; the use of wild-caught Cheetahs in this way goes back at least 4,300 years, and they were imported into Europe during the Renaissance. Nowadays, they are to be seen in most zoos and safari parks, but it is only recently (since 1960) that they have been successfully bred and even now only a few zoos are breeding them. They have lived for up to 19 years in captivity.

CALIFORNIAN SEA-LION
Zalophus californianus

The **Californian Sea-lion** is found along the Pacific coast of North America, and on the Galapagos Islands; it formerly occurred in Japanese waters but this population is now probably extinct. Sea-lions are frequently seen in zoos and as performing animals in circuses. They have good memories and, once tamed, will perform tricks even after a gap of several months. They were once extensively hunted for their skins, for oil, and for their blubber. They are relatively small, with males growing to about 8 ft. and females to 6 ft., and weigh up to 660lbs. and 220lbs. respectively. They have large eyes, small pointed ears and flippers which can be turned forwards, allowing them to gallop on land (unlike true seals). They are fast swimmers at up to 20 knots, and often "porpoise", swimming close to the surface and surfacing frequently. Females can jump up to 6 ft. clear of the water. After a gestation of about 340 days, they produce a single pup. They breed freely in captivity. Some have been released in the Mediterranean from time to time, where they may still live ferally. Several other species of sea-lion, and the closely related fur seals, are found throughout the north and east Pacific and the southern hemisphere. Some were once hunted to the verge of extinction, but fortunately have shown remarkable powers of recovery if properly protected.

WALRUS *Odobenus rosmarus*

A large bull **Walrus** can reach nearly 10 ft. long and weigh over 1 ton. The cows are much smaller but both sexes grow tusks which can be over 3 ft. long. The Walrus is an Arctic species, occurring around the Arctic coasts of Canada, Alaska and Russia; occasionally odd individuals stray southwards as far as Iceland or even Britain, where they were once regular visitors. They live mainly near the coast and feed on the sea bed on bivalve molluscs and crustaceans, diving to depths of over 230 ft. They have large flattened teeth for crushing molluscs, unlike other seals which have pointed teeth for eating fish. Stiff bristles on the muzzle

help locate prey in murky waters. Walrus live in herds, and are migratory, moving south for the winter and north during summer. A single calf is born after a gestation of about 11 months. It can swim soon after birth, but stays with its mother for about 2 years. Walrus live for up to about 30 years in the wild. They have always been of considerable economic importance to Arctic peoples, but during the 17th and 18th centuries commercial hunting for both ivory and oil exterminated many populations and reduced others. Walruses have been kept in many zoos, but only comparatively recently with success. One kept in New York Zoo ate over 130 lbs. of fish a day.

ELEPHANT SEALS

Elephant seals may weigh nearly as much as an elephant. A mature bull can reach over 3 tons in weight and over 16 ft. in length. There are 2 species. The **Southern Elephant Seal** *Mirounga leonina*, found on sub-Antarctic islands and the coast of Patagonia, is the larger. The **Northern Elephant Seal** *M. angustirostris* is confined to North America, centered around the Santa Barbara Islands and islands off California and Mexico. Both feed in deep water (up to 2000 ft. or more) and can dive for over 10 minutes. They eat a variety of fish which they swallow whole. To digest their prey they have a long gut, up to 650 ft. long.

Northern Elephant Seal

male female

Although Elephant Seals are mainly solitary at sea, during the breeding season they are very gregarious and crowd together, the males forming harems. Males start to develop their elephant-like proboscis when they are 2 years old, but it is not fully developed for about another 6 years. It is inflated only during the breeding season, when it may function as a resonator to amplify the male's roar when defending his territory. During the 19th century, both species were exploited for oil, and almost extinct by 1900. Under protection, they have largely recovered and are once again locally abundant. The Southern Elephant Seal is more common in zoos. It has occasionally bred in captivity, where one has lived for 15 years.

Southern Elephant Seal
males fighting

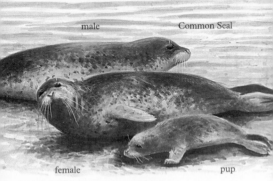

male   Common Seal

female   pup

COMMON SEAL *Phoca vitulina*

The **Common** or **Harbor Seal** is comparatively small, growing to a maximum of about 6½ ft. and a weight of 330 lbs. It is found in coastal waters in the north Atlantic and north Pacific and also in a number of freshwater lakes, including the Seal and Harrison Lakes in Quebec. The pups are born in spring or summer, often on sand banks at low tide, and can swim within a few hours of birth. They are suckled in the water until 3-4 weeks old, when they have to fend for themselves. It is usually these young animals which are found starving and brought to zoos. Common Seals can spend up to 20 minutes under water.

BAIKAL SEAL *Phoca sibirica*

The **Baikal Seal** is the world's smallest seal, growing to a maximum of about 4½ ft., and is the only one to be entirely confined to fresh water, in Lake Baikal, Siberia. The seals spend the winter beneath the ice of the frozen lake where the temperature of the water can be 100°F warmer than that of the air above. They keep breathing holes clear of ice, and in late winter the females emerge from the water to make dens in snowdrifts on the ice, where they give birth to 1 or 2 pups. The Baikal Seal is closely related to the **Ringed Seal** of the Arctic and to the **Caspian Seal**, and also to the **Larga** and **Common Seals,** some populations of which occur in land-locked waters. It has suffered in recent years from the increasing pollution of Lake Baikal by timber processing plants, and in the past has been hunted extensively for its pelt. Baikal Seals are now rarely seen in zoos outside Russia, although they were once popular exhibits.

Common Seal
floating

Baikal Seal

BOTTLE-NOSED DOLPHIN
Tursiops truncatus

The **Bottle-nosed Dolphin** is one of the most common and most widespread dolphins in the Atlantic, Indian, and South Pacific oceans. In the North Pacific it is replaced by a very closely related species, **Gills's Bottle-nosed Dolphin** *T. gilli*. As the name suggests, Bottle-nosed Dolphins have rather stubby snouts, and are variable in color, usually with dark grey on the back fading to white on the belly (which may have a pinkish flush). They grow to about 13 ft. and usually weigh up to 450 lbs. (occasionally as much as 1430 lbs.) and have tall, broad-based dorsal fins. Although frequently grouping together to form very large schools of up to 1,000 animals, more usually they occur in groups of between 3 and 15. Very sociable and playful by nature, they are often encountered riding the bow wave of boats, riding surf and can be seen jumping clear of the water. Like other dolphins they use sonar (echolocation) in order to navigate. The single calf is born after a gestation of approximately one year and is suckled for a further 12-18 months. Females reach maturity at 5-12 years, males 9-13 years old. Bottle-nosed Dolphins are the most popular species of dolphin to be exhibited in zoos and aquaria and were first successfully kept in captivity over a century ago. Although regularly bred in captivity, the majority are still wild-caught for zoos and aquaria.

KILLER WHALE *Orcinus orca*

The **Killer Whale** or **Orca**, is the largest of the dolphins, and often described as a "sea wolf" because of its predatory habits. Adult males grow to over 30 ft., females are smaller and less heavily built. In the sea their most distinctive characteristic is the large (up to 6 ft.), erect, triangular dorsal fin; for reasons not entirely understood, in captivity the dorsal fin is not so erect. They live in all oceans and adjoining seas, in groups which range in size from small family groups of 5-20 up to herds of 150 or more. They are very fast swimmers, reaching speeds of over 25 knots, and feed on a wide variety of marine animals including fish, squid, marine turtles, penguins, sea-birds, seals, sea-lions and whales and dolphins. Packs of Killer Whales hunt larger dolphins and whales up to the size of Minke and Grey Whale calves. However, there does not appear to be any authentic account of a Killer Whale attacking man without provocation, although divers wearing wetsuits must look remarkably like seals or dolphins. A single calf is born after a gestation of 13-16 months. Killer Whales are popular exhibits in zoos and aquaria, but as they are the largest cetacean normally kept in zoos, only a few have the necessary facilities. In captivity, they eat about 100 lbs. of fish a day. They are easily trained to perform a wide variety of "'tricks" and can often perform within 2 months of capture. Killer Whales are hunted in many parts of the world, and, although not endangered, have declined in many areas. In the wild, they can live to over 50 years.

FIN, BLUE AND SEI WHALES

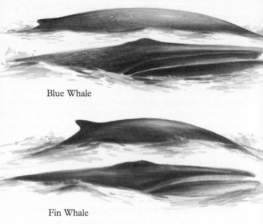

Blue Whale

Fin Whale

Sei Whale

The **Fin Whale** or **Common Rorqual** *Balaenoptera physalus* is one of the most common and most widespread of the great whales. Its numbers declined dramatically in the 1980s due to exploitation, but now that it is protected, the numbers are recovering and the population is estimated to be over 100,000. Found as far north as the Pacific, it has been recorded in the Baltic and Mediterranean. This slender whale is thought to be the fastest swimming of the great whales. They usually live in schools of up to 10 animals and sometimes come close to land. The Blue Whale *B. musculus* is the largest living animal, growing to a maximum length of over 100 ft., although they no longer reach the sized attained before exploitation. It is now very rare. The Sei (pronounced "say") Whale *B. borealis* occurs in all oceans and seas, except the colder, polar waters, and is a summer visitor to western Europe. It can be distinguished by its very sharply pointed fin and its habit of rising to the surface at a shallow angle so that the fin can often be seen at the same time as the head. The **Minke Whale** *B. acutorostrata* is the smallest of the rorquals, and is widely distributed in all oceans and seas; it is the only great whale that has ever been exhibited in captivity.

Minke Whale

HUMPBACK AND SPERM WHALES

Humpack Whale

Sperm Whale

The **Humpback Whale** *Megaptera novaeangliae* was once found in nearly all seas and oceans, and original populations were thought to number 15,000 in the northern hemisphere and 100,000 in the southern hemisphere. However, by the 1980s the world population was estimated to be less than 7,000 and is only slowly increasing due to protection. It is still threatened by accidental entanglement in fishing tackle and competition from commercial fisheries. It grows to over 50 ft., the flippers are relatively large (up to one-third of the body length) and the small dorsal fin is of variable shape. The head is covered in bumps and the edges of the whitish flippers are scalloped. Well-known for their vocalizations, this whale is extremely agile, often "breaching", leaping completely clear of the water, and plunging back headfirst, slapping its tail loudly.

The **Sperm Whale** or **Cachalot** *Physeter catodon* is widely distributed throughout the oceans, particularly in warmer waters. It is the largest of the toothed whales; the male grows to over 65 ft., the female is usually less than 36 ft. The head is enormous (containing the largest mammalian brain, weighing about 20 lbs.), with a squarish snout which projects well beyond the narrow jaw. It is usually found in groups of 20-40 (pods) which may aggregate on migration, when up to 3,000-4,000 have been seen. They have been hunted since 1712, mostly for their oil and the spermaceti wax from their heads, but also for ambergris (a gut product used in perfumery) and occasionally for meat.

MANATEES

American Manatee

There are 3 closely related species of manatee. The **American Manatee** *Trichechus manatus* which is found in coastal waters from Florida south through the Caribbean to Guyana, generally in water with a temperature of about 70°F. The **Amazon Manatee** *T. inunguis* occurs in the Amazon Basin and adjacent coastal waters; and the **African Manatee** *T. senegalensis* from coastal waters and rivers from Senegal to Angola. The related **Dugong** *Dugong dugong* occurs in the Indian Ocean and Australian waters. They all belong to the family Sirenia or Sea Cows and are entirely aquatic, browsing on aquatic plants. Because of their enormous appetites, they have been introduced into canals to clear them of choking water weeds such as water hyacinth. In captivity, the American Manatee eats 60-100 lbs. of vegetation a day. It can grow to a length of 15 ft. and a weight of 2,200 lbs., but is usually smaller. Manatees swim by moving their large spatulate tails up and down. A single calf is born under water after a gestation of about 1 year; is weaned at about 1 year, and is sexually mature at about 9 years. All manatees are threatened, and many populations endangered or even locally extinct. In the past, they were hunted for their meat and oil, and as recently as 1950, some 38,000 Amazon Manatees were killed in a single year. One of the main threats to the manatee in Florida and the Caribbean comes from boat propellors. Manatees are occasionally kept in zoos and aquaria but rarely breed. They have lived for over 30 years in captivity.

AFRICAN ELEPHANT
Loxodonta african

Within historic times, the **African Elephant** occurred almost throughout the length and breadth of Africa, except in the extreme desert regions of the Sahara and Namibia. It is the largest living land animal, standing up to 13 ft. at the shoulder, with a length of up to 24 ft. (including trunk), plus a tail of up to 4½ ft. It weighs up to 7½ tons, but usually less; males are larger than females. The trunk is a highly modified nose, and has a finger-like end which can be used to pick up food, and other objects. The ears of the African Elephant are up to 5 ft. long – much larger than those of the **Asiatic Elephant.** In many parts of their African distribution, numbers have been seriously depleted by ivory poaching and, although the trade in ivory is largely illegal, poaching continues to be the major threat to elephant populations. African Elephants live in groups led by females (cows), but may congregate into larger herds, especially at the approach of the rainy season. Mature males form separate herds, and old males may become solitary. A single young (occasionally twins) is born after a gestation of 22 months, weighing up to 300 lbs. The young is suckled for 2 years or more. They continue to grow for 25 or more years and their life expectancy is 50-70 years. They have been trained in similar ways to Asiatic Elephants; the war elephants of the Carthaginians, with which Hannibal crossed the Alps, were African Elephants, and in 1910 a training center was established in the Belgian Congo, which still exists in present-day Zaire. African Elephants, considered less trustworthy than Asiatic Elephants in captivity, are generally less popular as zoo animals.

ASIATIC OR INDIAN ELEPHANT
Elephas maxima

The Asiatic Elephant used to occur from Syria across Asia south of the Himalayas to China and Indochina and south to Sri Lanka, the Malay Peninsula and Sumatra. Its present range is considerably reduced: extinct west of India, it is still found in India, Sri Lanka, Thailand, Burma, Malaysia, China, Vietnam, Borneo, Sumatra, and a few adjacent areas. It is smaller than the **African Elephant**, standing up to 10 ft. at the shoulder, and growing to a total length (including trunk) of 21 ft., plus a tail of 5 ft., and weighing up to 11,000 lbs. The Asiatic Elephant has smaller ears than the African, and like the African it often carries tusks, which are modified upper incisors. Whereas both sexes of African Elephant usually have tusks, only the male normally has tusks in the Asiatic. It has been domesticated both for work in forestry, hunting and as a war animal (though this latter use is now purely ceremonial). However, they have not been truly domesticated, but rather wild animals are captured, tamed, and trained. A single calf is born after a gestation of up to 22 months, weighing up to 330 lbs; at birth the calf is covered in brownish hair, and even when adult they are often still sparsely haired. They reach sexual maturity when between 9 and 12 years old and a captive Asiatic Elephant has lived for 69 years. Like the African Elephant, the Asiatic has been hunted extensively for its ivory and it has been estimated that there may be fewer than 28,000 Asiatic Elephants left in their entire range.

WILD HORSE *Equus ferus*

The ancestor of domestic horses and ponies, the **Wild Horse** is thought to be extinct in the wild, although a few of the eastern race known as **Przewalski's Horse** *E. ferus przewalskii* may have survived until recently in Mongolia and Sinkiang. Przewalski's Horse is a rather heavily built, sandy colored horse with a stiff mane. At the turn of the century, some of these horses were captured and imported into Europe. They formed the basis of all the animals now in zoos, where there are thriving herds, and some of them are being reintroduced into the wild. Attempts have been made to recreate the western race, known as the Tarpan, by inbreeding primitive Polish Konik ponies, and these experiments have been successful in as much as the animals closely resemble the extinct Tarpan. Some of them have been released into semi-natural conditions in Poland.

ZEBRAS

There are 3 living species of zebra: the **Common Zebra** *Equus burchelli*, **Mountain Zebra** *E. zebra* and **Grevy's Zebra** *E. grevyi*. The fourth, the **Quagga** *E. quagga*, became extinct in 1883. All zebras are decreasing in numbers and give cause for conservation concern. The zebras are an exclusively African group of animals, the Common Zebra being found in open country from southern Ethiopia to South Africa and is one of the characteristic animals of the African plains. The Mountain Zebra is confined to montane areas of southern Africa, and Grevy's Zebra is reduced to three rather isolated populations in arid open areas near the borders of Ethiopia, Somalia, and Kenya. Zebras live in groups of 1 stallion with up to 6 mares, which may join together to form large herds. The single foal is born after a gestation of about 1 year and is active soon after birth. In captivity, Common Zebra have lived for up to 40 years.

Grevy's Zebra

WILD ASSES

The **African Wild Ass** *Equus africanus* is one of the rarest animals in the world. It was once found throughout most of the open areas of northern Africa, but is now confined to a few remote, arid parts of Somalia and Ethiopia, and in the 1970s, the world population was estimated to be no more than 3,000. Military activity coupled with prolonged drought will undoubtedly have had an adverse effect on its survival. It is the ancestor of the domesticated donkey *E. asinus* which has gone wild in many parts of the world, including parts of the Wild Ass's former range. Wild donkeys are also found in the southern USA where they are known as *burros*. Donkeys are also used in creating hybrids with horses which are known as mules. Mules are usually, though not necessarily, sterile.

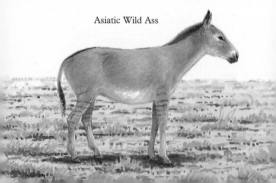

Asiatic Wild Ass

The **Kiang** *E. kiang* is the largest of the wild asses, characterised by its large head and "Roman" nose. The tail is tufted at the tip and the coat is long and thick. It occurs in the arid, inaccessible steppes of Tibet. The **Asiatic Wild Ass** *E. hemionus* is reduced to 4 separate populations, numbers having been drastically depleted by hunting for sport and food. Domestic donkeys have lived over 40 years in captivity but it is unlikely that asses live for more than 20 years in the wild.

Domesticated Donkey

WHITE OR SQUARE-LIPPED RHINOCEROS *Ceratotherium simum*

The White Rhinoceros formerly occurred in 2 separate parts of Africa: the **Northern White Rhino** *C.s. cottoni* below the Sahara from Chad to the Sudan and south to north-east Zaire and north-west Uganda; the Southern White Rhino *C.s. simum* in south-east Angola, south-west Zambia, Mozambique, Zimbabwe, Botswana and South Africa. It is now extinct over much of its range and very few of the Northern White survive. Under strict protection, the Southern White has flourished in South Africa and has been introduced into a number of national parks in Kenya and Zimbabwe, as well as being exported to zoos. The White Rhino is surpassed in size only by the elephant. A fully-grown bull can weigh up to 7920 lbs., stand over 6½ ft. at the shoulder and be up to 13 ft. long. They have 2 horns, of which the front one grows to about 3 ft., occasionally to over 5 ft.; females' horns are longer and thinner than those of males. The name White is derived from the Afrikaans *weit* meaning wide, referring to its square lip, the **Black Rhino** having a narrow pointed lip. White Rhinos are found in bush and savannah, usually with trees and access to water, where they feed mainly on short grass. The single calf is born after a gestation of about 16-18 months, suckled for about a year and remains with its mother for 2-3 years, leaving only when the next calf is born. A wild female has been recorded as breeding at 36 years of age. White Rhinos have no enemies other than man. Their present rarity is due mainly to poaching for their horn, highly prized in the Far East as a medicine powder, particularly for treating fevers, and in parts of Asia for carving. There are many Southern Whites in captivity, often breeding freely, but only a handful of the Northern subspecies.

powdered
rhino horn

143

BLACK RHINOCEROS *Diceros bicornis*

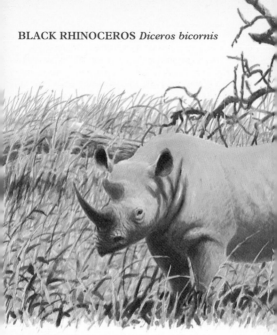

The **Black Rhino** was at one time widespread throughout Africa south of the Sahara but, outside East Africa, is now restricted to a few isolated and scattered populations. In the last few years, many East African populations have also been exterminated and most of those surviving are under considerable poaching pressure. The Black Rhino grows to a maximum length of 12 ft., a shoulder height of 7½ ft. and a weight of 3,520 lbs.; the front of 2 horns grows to a length of up to 2½ ft., sometimes 4 ft. Almost exclusively a browser, the Black Rhino's pointed and prehensile lip, which it uses to grasp the leaves of bushes and shrubs, distinguishes it from the **White Rhino**, which is a grazer. Black Rhinos live in quite thickly wooded country, forest edges and more open shrub and thorn country, usually close to a permanent water supply. Like other rhinos, they are rather short-sighted and rely on their senses of hearing and smell, often charging unknown sounds and scents; but they usually avoid humans and may run off at speeds of up to 30 mph. The single calf is born after a gestation of about 15 months. It suckles for up to a year but also eats solid food regularly from about one month old, and stays with the cow until the next young is born. Black Rhino have lived for over 45 years in the wild. As with other rhinos, the shape and size of the horns vary and can be used to identify individuals. Black Rhino have long been poached for their horns, many of which were smuggled from Africa to the Middle East to be carved into dagger handles.

Jambia with a rhino horn handle

145

ASIAN RHINOCEROS

Indian Rhino

Sumatran Rhino

Javan Rhino

The 3 species of Asian Rhinoceros are much rarer than the African species and considered endangered. Only the **Indian Rhino** *Rhinoceros unicornis* is normally seen in zoos. Once found over much of northern India, Nepal, Assam, and northern Pakistan, it is now confined to a few reserves, of which the most important are Kaziranga in Assam and Chitawan in Nepal. Indian Rhinos grow to a length of 14 ft., a shoulder height of 6½ ft. and a weight of up to 880 lbs. Easily distinguished from African rhinos by their skin, which hangs in loose armor-like folds, they live in tall grass and swampy jungles, rarely going far from water, in which they wallow. The single young is born after a gestation of about 16 months. Its life span is estimated at 50 years or more.

The **Javan Rhino** *R. sondaicus*, closely related to, though much smaller than, the Indian Rhino, was once fairly widespread from eastern India to southern China, south to Java. Now one of the most endangered of all animals, the only certain survivors are in the Udjung Kulon Reserve, Java.

The **Sumatran** or **Hairy Rhino** *Dicerorhinus sumatrensis*, once found from Assam and Bengal to Vietnam and south to Borneo, now occurs only in small, scattered populations over a much reduced range. Its front horn is inconspicuous and the second horn also rather short. No Sumatran or Javan Rhinos are currently in zoos but the only hope for their survival may depend on some being captured to start a captive breeding program.

TAPIRS

Malayan Tapir

Brazilian Tapir

There are 4 species of tapir, 3 of which are found in tropical South America and one in south-east Asia. They are hoofed mammals, related to horses and rhinoceros, having an uneven number of toes. Tapirs are mainly browsers, feeding on leaves and shoots and also on aquatic vegetation, and occasionally graze on crops. All 4 species are exhibited in zoos and have been bred in captivity. The most commonly exhibited tapirs are the Malayan and the Brazilian. The most widespread of the South American species is the **Brazilian Tapir** *Tapirus terrestris* which is found from Colombia and Venezuela south to southern Brazil and Argentina. **Baird's Tapir** *T. bairdi* is found from Mexico south to Ecuador and the **Mountain Tapir** *T. roulini (= pinchaque)* in the Andes from Colombia to northern Peru, at altitudes above 6500 ft. (2000 m). The number of both Baird's and Mountain Tapir are declining.

The **Malayan Tapir** *T. indicus* is found from Burma, south through Thailand and the Malay Peninsula to Sumatra; it is now very rare over most of its range. The Malayan Tapir grows to a length of up to about 7½ ft. (the tail is insignificant) and weighs up to 825 lbs. A single calf is born after a gestation of about 390 days and, like the Brazilian Tapir, it is heavily striped. The females probably give birth in alternate years, and in captivity a male has lived to over 30 years of age. In the wild tapirs are often hunted for food and they have also become rare as their forest habitats have been cleared for agriculture.

HYRAXES

Cape Dassie

Tree Hyrax

The 5 living species of hyrax or dassie are quite unlike any other mammal and placed in their own order, Hyracoidea. They are often described as being closely related to elephants – in reality it is likely that both elephants and hyraxes share a common ancestor. They are mostly found in Africa, but have also spread into the mediterranean area, and are the Conies mentioned in the Bible (Proverbs Ch. XXX, verse 26).

The hyrax most frequently seen in zoos is the **Cape Dassie** or **Large-toothed Rock Hyrax** *Procavia capensis*. It is widespread in most open habitats in Africa south of the Sahara and also northwards to Egypt, the Levant and Arabia. It grows to a length of up to 2 ft., and a weight of 11 lbs. Dassies inhabit rocky hillsides, ravines, and kloofs (or gorges), where they are colonial. They do not move far from cover and emerge in the morning and evening to sunbathe. They have look-out points from which the alarm call is whistled, and also well-used walkways and easily recognized latrine areas. Up to 6 young are born fully furred with their eyes open, after a gestation of about 240 days, and are active within a day of birth. They suckle for up to 5 months, but leave the breeding hole after 3 months, and are not normally sexually mature until their second year. They are preyed on by a wide range of animals, including Leopards and other cats, eagles, and large snakes. In areas where Leopards and other predators have been exterminated, dassies have increased to pest proportions, damaging crops. They make active and interesting exhibits in zoos, where they often breed fairly freely and have lived for up to 12 years. The 3 species of tree hyrax *Dendrohyrax* are inhabitants of the African forests and are much more solitary animals, remaining concealed during the day and emerging at night to feed.

AARDVARK *Orycteropus afer*

The **Aardvark** or **Ant Bear** has a wide range in Africa, south of the Sahara, occuring almost everywhere with a suitable habitat, although in recent years it has declined in many areas. It grows to a length of up to 5 ft., plus a tapering tail of up to 2 ft., and it weighs up to 175 lbs. Aardvarks have evolved several modifications to enable them to dig for termites; they have powerful claws, the nostrils at the end of the long snout are protected by stiff hairs and the long tubular ears can be folded back. Aardvarks are nocturnal, and spend the day in a tunnel which they excavate, blocking the entrance except for an air vent. Although they feed mainly on termites, they also take other

insects and their larvae and the fungi which grows in termite colonies. They also seek out wild cucumbers, the seeds of which need to be partly digested before they can germinate. A single young (occasionally twins) is born in a nest in a burrow after a gestation of 7 months, and is pink and hairless at birth. After about 2 weeks the young accompanies the mother foraging, and after about 6 months the young starts digging for itself. In captivity, an aardvark has lived for 23 years.

The abandoned burrows of aardvarks provide homes and shelter for a wide range of other wildlife including bats, ground squirrels, porcupines, monitor lizards, pythons, jackals, hyenas, and owls. Although their thick skins protect them from termite and other insect bites, aardvarks have many enemies, particularly when young; they are preyed on by leopards, lions, hyenas, hunting dogs and even pythons. When attacked they usually try to run away or dig themselves into the ground, but an aardvark will also defend itself with its forefeet. Aardvarks are comparatively unusual in zoos, but have been bred on several occasions, and for more than one generation.

WILD BOAR *Sus scrofa*

The **Wild Boar**, the ancestor of the domestic pig, was once found over most of Europe, North Africa and eastwards across to Japan and southeast Asia. In its domestic forms, it has also been extensively introduced or has escaped; feral and wild pigs now occur in New Guinea, New Zealand, many oceanic islands and some parts of Africa, North, and South America. Wild Boar grow up to 6 ft. long, stand 3 ft. at the shoulder and weigh up to 500 lbs.; males (boars) are larger than females (sows), and have protruding tusks which can grow to 1 ft. Wild Boar occur in a wide variety of usually wooded habitats, and eat mainly vegetable foods. They often feed on man's crops and can cause extensive damage. They are hunted for sport and in many parts of their range (notably Britain) have been exterminated. Wild Boar normally live alone or in small groups ("sounders"), but sometimes in groups of 100 or more. They are mainly active at night and twilight, hiding in dense cover by day. In spring or early summer, after a gestation of about 140 days, a litter of up to 12 piglets is born in a rough nest built by the mother which they leave after a few days. They are weaned at 3-4 months and become sexually mature at 8-10 months. In Thailand, they may have been domesticated nearly 12,000 years ago. The domestic pigs of Europe were often very boar-like until the 18th century, when they were cross-bred with oriental pigs. The introduction of domestic pigs on to oceanic islands has been responsible for the decline and even extinction of many species; the most famous is the Dodo of Mauritius. Wild Boar are often exhibited in zoos and many live for up to 20 years in captivity.

WARTHOG *Phacochoerus aethiopicus*

The **Warthog** is widespread in suitable habitat over most of Africa, south of the Sahara. Its preferred habitat includes woodlands, savannahs, scrub and swamps and it also occurs in more open plains and mountainous habitats up to 8125 ft. (2500 m). The Warthog grows to 5 ft., plus a tail of 18 in., and weighs up to 330 lbs; the male is larger than the female and has longer tusks, growing up to 2 ft. Unlike most other pigs they, are mainly active during the daytime. They feed mainly on vegetable matter including roots and rhizomes, grasses, fruits and berries and, occasionally carrion. They live in small groups which may band together to form much larger groups of up to 40. Adult males are usually solitary, only joining females for mating, when they fight other males. These fights are rit-

ualized: they strike each other with their head, the fleshy head warts softening the blows. After a gestation of up to 175 days, a litter of 2-4 (occasionally up to 8) is born in a burrow. At 7 weeks, the young accompany the mother. In captivity, a Warthog has lived for over 18 years. Although Warthogs are one of the commonest pigs in Africa, they are not all that often seen in zoos, and only breed infrequently in captivity.

Three other species of wild pig are found in Africa: the Wild Boar (p.154), the **Bush Pig** *Potamochoerus porcus* and the **Giant Forest Hog** *Hylochoerus meinertzhageni*. The Bush Pig (or Red River Hog) is sometimes exhibited in zoos. It is found in more forested areas than the Warthog, over much of Africa, south of the Sahara. The Bush Pig has recently increased with the spread of agriculture (it often feeds on crops) and the extermination of predators such as the leopard. The Giant Forest Hog was one of the last large mammals to be discovered in Africa. It grows to a length of up to 6 ft., stands up to 3 ft. high at the shoulder and weighs up to 550 lbs. It is found in forests from Liberia to Kenya and southern Ethiopia, but its range is still not properly known, nor much known of its habits.

PECCARIES

Collared Peccary

The peccaries are the New World equivalents of the pigs. There are 3 species: the **Collared Peccary** *Tayassu tajacu*, which is the most widespread, occurring from the southern states of the USA, south through Central and South America to northern Argentina; the **White-lipped Peccary** *Tayassu pecari* which occurs in forests from southern Mexico south to northern Argentina and the Chaco Peccary *Catagonus wagneri*, which was only discovered as a living animal in the 1970s, and is confined to the Gran Chaco area on the borders of Bolivia, Paraguay, and Argentina. The Collared Peccary lives in a wide variety of habitats including semi-desert, rain forest and swamps. They grow to a length of just under 3 ft. (the tail of about 1 in. is not easily visible), stand up to 2 ft. at the shoulder and weigh up to 60 lbs., usually less. They are social animals, living in mixed age and sex groups of 2-15, occasionally up to 50. They search for food among forest litter and soil with their snout and can smell food even when it is several inches below the surface. They feed mostly on plant matter including cacti fruit, grasses, seeds, and nuts, and only occasionally animals or carrion are eaten. The female produces a litter of 1-4 (usually 2) after a gestation of 115 days, in a nest under a log or in a burrow. Within a few days they follow their mother when she rejoins the herd. The young mature rapidly and in captivity they are capable of breeding when they are only 33 weeks old, but in the wild they are nearly a year old when they first breed. Collared Peccaries are exhibited in many zoos, and they are frequently bred in captivity and have been bred for many generations.

HIPPOPOTAMI

The **Hippopotamus** *Hippopotamus amphibius* was once widely distributed in Africa south of the Sahara in almost all areas with suitable aquatic habitats. Within historic times it occurred in the Nile (and was often depicted by the Ancient Egyptians) and during the Pleistocene Period was found as far north as southern England. Although its range is now considerably reduced and fragmented, it is locally abundant. Hippos grow to a length of up to 15 ft., a shoulder height of 5 ft., and a weight of 9900 lbs. Canine teeth, enlarged into "tusks", may weigh 7 lbs., and are often used as a substitute for elephant or walrus ivory. Hippos spend most of the day sleeping submerged in water with only ears, eyes and nostrils exposed. At night, they leave the water to graze and may travel 2 miles or more to grazing sites. Normally harmless, Hippos can be dangerous if their retreat to water is cut off. They breed at all times of the year; the single calf (rarely twins) is born after a gestation of up to 8 months. The new-born calves can swim before they can walk, and suckle under water. In the wild, the average life span when not hunted by man is 41 years. They breed regularly in captivity.

The **Pygmy Hippopotamus** *Choeropsis liberiensis* is restricted to isolated areas in West Africa, from Sierra Leone to Nigeria. Very much smaller than the Hippopotamus, it grows to a maximum length of 5½ ft., a height of 3 ft., and a weight of 600 lbs. It is less aquatic and found mainly near streams and rivers in wet forests and swamps. The Pygmy Hippo is comparatively rare in the wild and classified as vulnerable but there is a substantial zoo population, mostly bred in captivity, where one has lived for over 38 years.

Pygmy Hippopotamus

CAMELS

There are two species of Camel: the **Dromedary** or **Arabian Camel** *Camelus dromedarius* and the **Bactrian Camel** *C. ferus* (= *bactrianus*). They live in arid areas where they can survive for long periods without drinking, obtaining moisture from vegetation, including salty plants. They can drink as much as 15 gallons to replenish their body fluids. The female usually gives birth to a single calf (rarely twins) every other year after a gestation of up to 440 days. The young are fully independent at 4 years old and fully grown at 5. They can live up to 50 years. Camels grow to about 11 ft. 6 in. long, a shoulder height of 7 ft. and a weight of 1,520 lbs. They have a characteristic rolling gait, caused by moving the fore and hind legs together on each side; they can run at 40 mph.

Dromedary

The single-humped Dromedary was domesticated perhaps as early as 4000 BC. The wild form, found in Arabia and possibly North Africa, either became extinct nearly 2,000 years ago or was gradually absorbed into the domestic herds. Dromedaries have been introduced into many parts of the world, including southern USA, south and east Africa, Spain and Australia (where a large feral population still exists).

The Bactrian or Two-humped Camel is well-adapted to living in sandy desert and other arid environments, having thick eyelashes, nostrils which can be closed to keep out sand, and broad feet. They feed on almost any vegetation and can survive without water for extended periods. It once ranged from Turkestan to the gobi Desert but its range is now restricted to two small areas of the Gobi in south-western Mongolia and western China. Less than 500 animals are thought to survive.

Bactrian Camel

GUANACO AND VICUNA

The **Guanaco** *Lama guanicoe* is thought to be the wild ancestor of both the **Llama** *L. glama* and the **Alpaca** *L. pacos*. They inhabit dry, open countryside from southern Peru to eastern Argentina and south to Tierra del Fuego. They grow to a length of 7½ ft., and a shoulder height of 4 ft. The **Vicuna** *Vicugna vicugna*, smaller and more lightly built than the Guanaco and its domesticated relatives, is found in the Andes of southern Peru, Argentina, Bolivia and Chile, in rather arid grasslands. They usually live in small groups, consisting of a male, several females and their offspring, or in batchelor herds, in territories of up to 75 acres. They are unique among hoofed animals in so far as their lower incisor teeth grow continuously, and have enamel only on one side. By the 1960s, Vicuna numbers were down to less than 10,000, mainly due to hunting for their valuable wool, but subsequent pro-

Llamas

Guanacos

tection has enabled them to recover and there are now probably over 80,000. The Alpaca and Llama have been domesticated for about 4,500 years; the Alpaca is bred mainly for its wool while the Llama is primarily a beast of burden. Llamas will interbreed with Guanaco and Alpaca and consequently many different varieties have been bred, but it is likely that they will become increasing rare as motorised transport becomes more widely available.

RED DEER OR WAPITI *Cervus elaphus*

stag

hind

In the Old World, the **Red Deer** is widespread throughout most of Europe and across Asia to Siberia, China and Korea, and south to the Himalayas and North Africa. In North America, where it is known as the **Elk** or **Wapiti**, it is widespread in southern Canada and most of the USA. It has also been introduced into New Zealand and other parts of the world. There is considerable variation in size, largely depending on the quality of the habitat. Animals from New Zealand, parts of North America and the Carpathians are among the largest, growing to a shoulder height of 5 ft., a length of 8½ ft. and a weight of up to 750 lbs. However, from other parts of their range, such as the Highlands of Scotland, Red Deer are often considerably smaller, weighing as little as 175 lbs. They are gregarious, each sex forming separate herds for most of the year. Their preferred habitat is open woodlands, but they are very adaptable. A single calf (occasionally twins) is born after a gestation of up to 9 months, is active soon after birth, and follows the mother when about 3 days old. It is heavily spotted at birth, but molts by about 3 months.

Wapiti stag in winter

PÈRE DAVID'S DEER *Elaphurus davidianus*

Père David's Deer originally occurred in the lowlands of northeast China, but became extinct in the wild nearly 3,000 years ago. However, a herd survived enclosed in the Imperial Hunting Park near Peking until 1900. In 1865, the French missionary and naturalist Father David (after whom the deer is named) was the first European to see them, and later he was able to send some live specimens to Europe where they were dispersed among several zoos. In 1894, a flood breached the walls of the Imperial Hunting Park and the deer escaped, only to be eaten by starving peasants. Six years later, most of the remainder were shot by foreign troops during the Boxer Rebellion, by 1911 only two were left in China and by 1921 both were dead. Meanwhile, the Duke of Bedford had gathered together as many as he could at his private zoo at Woburn, England. In 1900 and 1901, he gathered 16, and by 1922

rutting males

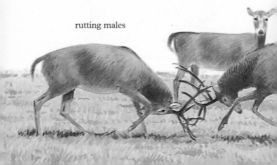

his herd had grown to 64. After World War II, the Woburn herd had grown large enough to allow others to be established, and by the early 1960s, the world total exceeded 400 and four were sent back to China. By the 1980s, there were over 1,000 dispersed among about 100 collections.

Père David's Deer grows to about 5 ft., stands about 3 ft. 9 in. at the shoulder and weighs about 440 lbs. They have large, spreading hooves, an adaptation to their original swampy habitat. During the rut the males fight with their antlers and teeth and also rear up on their hind legs and box. One or 2 fawns are born after a gestation of up to 270 days, and maturity is reached at about 27 months. Since its original habitat has completely disappeared, it is unlikely that it will ever be possible to release Père David's Deer into truly wild conditions.

male with antlers
shedding velvet

MOOSE OR ELK *Alces alces*

male with antlers
in velvet

Known in North America as the **Moose**, and in Europe as the **Elk**, this, the largest of the deer, is found in wooded areas that are covered with snow in winter, throughout the northern parts of the Old and New World. The Moose grows to 10 ft. long, standing up to 7 ft. 8 in. at the shoulder and weighing up to 1,800 lbs, but usually much less. The males carry broad palmate antlers, which grow to a record spread of over 6½ ft., and may weigh up to 80 lbs. Moose prefer fairly wet habitats, browsing on sallows and willows, and also on aquatic vegetation, eating nearly 40 lbs. a day. They are generally solitary but males will fight for females during the rut in September-October. After a gestation of up to 264 days, 1 or 2 (rarely 3) young are born which stay with the mother for at least a year. They have lived up to 27 years. In the past, the range of the Moose was considerably reduced by hunting and it had disappeared from most of Europe and much of the USA. However, under strict protection, its numbers have recovered and its range is still spreading – there were an estimated 2 million in the world by the 1970s. Moose are an important game animal and in Sweden provide a significant part of the national meat production. In Sweden during the last century, and more recently in the former USSR, they have been domesticated both for meat and milk, and have also been used as draft animals for pulling carts and sledges.

female

REINDEER OR CARIBOU
Rangifer tarundus

The **Reindeer,** or **Caribou** as it is known in North America, was once found throughout the more northerly latitudes of the northern hemisphere on Arctic tundra and in woodlands, but in many of the latter areas it is now extinct. In Europe, the wild reindeer is extinct in Norway and Sweden and endangered in Finland. Within historic times it also occurred in Poland and

Germany. Reindeer grow up to 7 ft. long, with a tail of up to 8 in., a shoulder height of 4½ ft., and a maximum weight of 700 lbs.; males are larger than females. They are the only deer in which both sexes have antlers, which are very variable and grow up to 4 ft. 3 in. long in males. They have broad, deeply cloven hooves which help when walking on soft snow and marshy ground – when running they can reach speeds of up to 50 mph. Most Reindeer are migratory, in the summer they move in herds to the northern latitudes, where the calves are born after a gestation of about 228 days. The single calf follows the mother an hour after birth, and a day later can run faster than a human. Throughout the Arctic regions Reindeer are hunted by the native peoples and in the Old World have been domesticated for about 3,000 years. Even when domesticated, most Reindeer continue to migrate between the summer and winter feeding grounds. Although wild Reindeer are threatened in many parts of their range, there are probably more than 3 million domesticated animals. They have been introduced into the Cairngorms (Scotland), South Georgia, the Kerguelen Islands, Iceland and Greenland. Their maximum life span in the wild is about 13 years, but a Reindeer has lived for over 20 years in captivity.

domesticated female
Reindeer and
Laplander

173

WHITE-TAILED DEER
Odicoileus virginianus

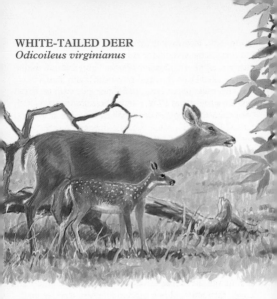

The **White-tailed Deer** is widespread over much of the Americas from southern Canada southwards to Peru and northern Brazil, and has been introduced into New Zealand, Cuba, and other parts of North America. In the western parts of its range it overlaps with or is replaced by the **Mule** or **Black-tailed Deer**, *O. hermionus*. The White-tailed Deer grows to a length of about 8 ft., stands up to 3 ft., and weighs up to 420 lbs However, there is considerable variation and these maxima apply to the subspecies *O. virginianus borealis*. The Florida Keys White-tailed Deer *O.v. clavium* is usually less than 55 lbs. This deer was once considered threatened with perhaps only 30 surviving in 1949, but under protection they had recovered to a population of 300-400 by 1980. White-tailed Deer live in a wide variety of habitats, usually with some cover in which to hide. They browse and graze on a variety of vegetable matter, including grass, herbs, fungi, lichen, bark, and twigs. By 1900, its US population had been reduced to about 500,000 but, under protection and management, it has risen to over 12 million, and about 2 million are killed each year by sport hunters. They rarely gather in large herds, but live in small family groups. Males do not form harems or defend territories, but move on once they have mated with a female. After a gestation of about 200 days, twins are usually born (except the first pregnancy which is usually a single young); occasionally there are 3 or 4 young in a litter. For the first month the female leaves the young hidden in dense cover, they start nibbling vegetation when a few days old, can run at about 3 weeks and are weaned by about 4 months. Young males are independent by about 1 year, but females usually remain with the mother for 2 years. Both White-tailed and Black-tailed Deer are successfully bred in captivity and have lived for up to 20 years. In some areas they are causing damage to the vegetation and are in need of culling.

GIRAFFE
Giraffe camelopardalis

The Giraffe once occurred in most of the open country of Africa, but since about AD 600 has been restricted to areas south of the Sahara and in the past 100 years has been exterminated in most of western and southern Africa. Several different color forms occur within the species. The Giraffe is the tallest living animal and a male grows to a maximum height of

Masai Giraffe

17½ ft., with a shoulder height of up to 12 ft., and a weight of up to 1800 lbs, but usually less; females are slightly smaller than males. Because of the enormous length of the neck, and to prevent blood rushing to the head when the giraffe is drinking, there is a series of valves in the blood vessels. Giraffes are browsers, feeding on leaves, buds and shoots, particularly those of acacias. Herds usually consist of females and young or batchelor herds; older bulls are usually solitary, wandering from herd to herd. The single young is born after a gestation of about 457 days; it is able to stand about 20 minutes after birth, and is soon walking. It is suckled for up to 13 months and remains with its mother for 4-5 months more. Giraffes can run at speeds of over 30 mph and have few enemies other than man, although Lion occasionally attack the young. They are bred regularly in captivity and have lived for over 36 years; the greatest age known in the wild is 26 years.

Rothschild's Giraffe

Reticulated Giraffe

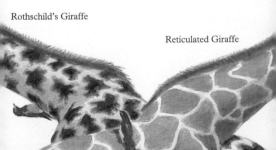

OKAPI *Okapia johnstoni*

The **Okapi** was one of the last large mammals to be discovered by Europeans, although it had long been known to the pygmies of the Congo. In 1900, Sir Harry Johnston (after whom it was named), a British naturalist and the Governor of Uganda, sent two strips of striped skin to the British Museum. Soon after he was able to send two skulls and a skin, and it was then realized that his discovery was closely related to the giraffe. In 1918, the first live Okapi was exhibited in Europe. The Okapi is a forest dwelling giraffe, found only in the Zaire (Congo) River basin. They live alone, in pairs or in small family groups, browsing on the leaves, fruit and seeds of a wide variety of plants. They are mainly active by day, and use well trodden paths, but disappear into dense undergrowth when alarmed.

Okapis grow to a length of about 7 ft., a shoulder height of 5½ ft. and a weight of 550 lbs. The males have small horns covered in hair. Living in dark forests, Okapis have relatively poor eyesight (though their exceptionally long tongue can be used to clean the eyes), but have large ears and acute hearing. The single young is born after a gestation of up to about 490 days, and in captivity an Okapi has lived for over 33 years. A captive female gave birth to 12 young, the last when she had reached an age of 26 years. Okapis now breed regularly in captivity, and most of those in zoos were bred in captivity. Although they are probably fairly rare, they are not thought to be in any immediate danger.

PRONGHORN *Antilocapra americana*

Pronghorn were once found widely in North America from Saskatchewan south to northern Mexico, and are still found in scrub, semi-desert, and grassland habitats within that range. They grow up to 5 ft. long, a shoulder height of 3 ft. and a weight of up to 155 lbs.; males are slightly larger than females. Both sexes carry horns which are unusual in that they consist of a central bone core, similar to that of cattle and sheep, and an outer keratinous (horn) casing which is shed annually. They are both browsers and grazers, feeding on grasses, herbs, bushes, cacti and other plants, and can survive without water. Pronghorns are usually gregarious; young males form bachelor herds, and older males hold territories. The females move about in groups. Fawns (1 at the first birth, twins thereafter) are born in spring after a gestation of about 252 days. They are sexually mature by 15-16 months and in captivity have lived for over 11 years. Outside the breeding season the herds often link up and form large aggregations of all ages and sexes – up to 1,000 have been recorded. These herds sometimes move at speeds of nearly 30 mph and a record of 54 mph has been recorded. Before Europeans arrived in America there were an estimated 35 million Pronghorns, by the 1920s there were 13,000. Under protection their numbers have risen to about half a million, and about 40,000 are killed each year by sport hunters. However, the southern populations are still endangered and the **Lower California Pronghorn**, *A. americana peninsularis*, restricted to southern Baja California, is considered endangered. In the 1920s there were 500, but by the late 1970s there were only about 80. The **Sonoran Pronghorn** *A. a. sonoriensis* from the Sonoran Desert, with a population of less than 450, is also considered endangered. It is not decreasing in the USA, but in Mexico has dropped by over 60 per cent in the last 25 years. They are rarely seen in zoos outside North America.

BONGO *Tragelaphus euryceros*

The forest-dwelling **Bongo** is confined to West Africa, Zaire, Kenya and Ethiopia and is quite rare in all those countries. They grow to about 8 ft. long, 4½ ft. at the shoulder and weigh up to 485 lbs. They usually live near water and wallow in mud holes. Both sexes have spiral horns which may be over 3 ft. long and when alarmed they charge through dense undergrowth with their horns laid back over their shoulders. Their diet consists of a wide variety of vegetation, but they mainly browse on bamboo, cassava, and sweet potato. They sometimes raid agricultural crops such as coco yams.

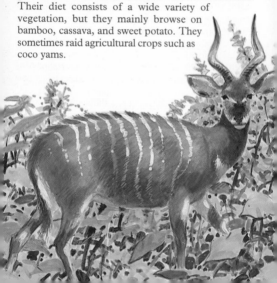

ELANDS

The 2 closely related species of eland occur only in Africa. The **Common Eland** *Tragelaphus oryx* was once found throughout Africa south from Ethiopia and southern Zaire, except in dense forest and arid desert areas. However, excessive hunting, loss of habitat and outbreaks of rinderpest, have eliminated it from much of its former range. They have been bred successfully in captivity, mainly for their high quality meat, but also because they are capable of living in conditions under which cattle do not thrive. The **Giant Eland** or **Lord Derby's Eland** *T. derbianus* was also once widespread, in a belt running south of the Sahara from Senegal to the southern Sudan, but is now divided into well-separated populations.

Giant Eland

ASIATIC WATER BUFFALO *Bubalis arnee*

The **Asiatic Water Buffalo** found in India is the wild ancestor of the domestic **Water Buffalo** *Bubalis bubalis* which has been widely introduced elsewhere by man. In the wild, the Water Buffalo is usually found in wet meadows, swamps, and overgrown river valleys where they feed on the lush vegetation at the water's edge. Domesticated Water Buffalo are primarily beasts of burden and are used for ploughing and tilling rice paddies. They also produce rich milk and excellent leather and become extremely tame. Despite the fact that it has been estimated that Water Buffalo numbers could be as high as 75 million worldwide, they are thought to be threatened in the wild.

WILD YAK *Bos mutus*

The **Yak,** one of the smaller species of cattle, is found in the bleak steppes close to the snow-line in the Tibetan plateau, north of the Himalayas. It is insulated against the extreme cold by fringes of shaggy hair beneath which there is an underfur of soft matted hair which is shed in spring. The Wild Yak is increasingly rare in its native habitat and although protected is still hunted. The **Domestic Yak** *B. grunniens* is used as a beast of burden, and for its wool and hair (which is very strong and good for making rugs), for the rich milk it produces, and also for its meat and leather.

The **European Bison** or **Wisent** *Bison bonasus* was once widespread and abundant. However, it disappeared from most of its range in prehistoric times and by the 1920s it was totally extinct in the wild. Fortunately, there were a number of animals in captivity which were subsequently bred enabling a herd to be reintroduced into the Bialowieza Forest in Poland and others have since been released into semi-natural conditions in other reserves in Poland, Russia and Romania. The **American Bison** *B. bison*, also known in North America as the Buffalo although it is not a true Buffalo, was once the most abundant large mammal on the entire continent, with an estimated 50 million ranging from Alaska to Mexico.

American Bison (male)

Destruction of large herds of Bison began with the first European colonists in North America, for although up to that time, many Indian tribes had been almost totally dependent on the Bison, they had never posed a serious threat to them. By 1890, less than 1,000 survived in the whole of North America. Fortunately the pioneer American conservationist, William Hornaday, led a campaign to save them and today there are over 50,000. The Yellowstone National Park is the only place in the USA in which Bison have lived continuously, but they have now been widely reintroduced into their former range.

187

WHITE OR ARABIAN ORYX *Oryx leucoryx*

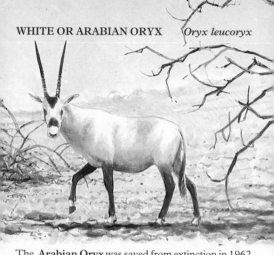

The **Arabian Oryx** was saved from extinction in 1962 when some of the last oryx were captured and breeding programs started up in the USA. The last wild oryx was probably killed in 1972. By the 1980s, there were over 150 in captivity and some were reintroduced into reserves in Jordan, Oman and Israel and those in Oman later released. There have also always been many in captivity in Arabia. The oryx is probably behind the legend about unicorns, possibly because the Romans used to bind their horns together so that they grew to look like a single horn.

BLACKBUCK *Antilope cervicapra*

The **Blackbuck** was once probably the most abundant hoofed animal in India, occuring in the open plains and scrub areas of India and Pakistan in herds of thousands. Now they are usually in herds of up to 50 and are comparatively rare having been extensively hunted by man, using Cheetahs and later guns. The females and young are led by a mature male, which usually has striking black coloration, although in the south of India they tend to be dark brown rather than black. A rarer Indian antelope is the **Four-horned Antelope** or **Chowsingha** *Tetracerus quadricornis* which was once found in open wooded country throughout most of the Indian peninsula. It is the only species of Bovidae to have 4 horns, although some domestic sheep have been bred with extra horns (such as Jacob's sheep).

male

female

SPRINGBOK *Antidorcas marsupialis*

The **Springbok** (or Springbuck) is the national emblem of the Republic of South Africa and was once one of the most numerous gazelles in Africa. It is now found in isolated populations in southern Africa. When European colonists first moved north from the Cape colony, across the veldt, they found huge migrating herds of Springbok which numbered several million individuals and took several days to pass by. Even though their numbers are now greatly reduced, herds of up to 1,500 occasionally occur. The last great trek of Springbok was in 1896 and spread over an area 15 miles wide and 140 miles long. Like Lemming migrations in the Arctic, Springbok treks often ended at the sea where tens of thousands died on the coast. Springbok take their name from their habit of high, vertical bouncing or leaping (spronking) when agitated; these leaps may be repeated many times. When alarmed they can run at speeds of up to 56 mph (90 kph) and make single leaps of 50 ft., in order to escape predators. They are preyed on by lions, leopards, hyenas and cheetah and the young are taken by smaller cats, jackals and eagles. The single young (rarely twins) is born after a gestation of up to 171 days. Substantial numbers occur in national parks. They are regularly bred in captivity, and have lived for up to 19 years. They grow to a length of 4 ft. 7 in. plus a tail of up to 11 in., stand up to 3 ft. at the shoulder and weigh up to 80 lbs.; the males are slightly larger than females and both sexes carry horns. The males have horns of up to 19 in., females up to 11 in.

CHAMOIS *Rupicapra rupicapra*

The **Chamois,** whose soft Chamois, or "shammy", leather is used for cleaning glass and other highly polished surfaces, is native to the mountains of southern Europe, Asia Minor and the Caucasus. Females and young (lambs) normally live in small herds of up to 30 animals, and they are joined by adult males in winter. In the past, over-hunting for their highly prized flesh, their horns, which were sought-after trophies, and their thick winter fur, which was used to make tufts known as gamsbart to adorn Tyrolean hats, has led to the local extermination of Chamois, particularly in the European part of its range. They have been released into New Zealand and are now well-established. The Appenine subspecies of Chamois *R. rupicapra ornata* is found only in the Abruzzo National Park in Italy where less than 500 survive.

Chamois in winter pelage and Alpine Chough

MUSK OX *Ovibos moschatus*

By the 1930s, **Musk Oxen** had declined to about 500 individuals, all on the Canadian mainland. But conservation measures have allowed them to increase significantly and it is estimated that they now number over 25,000. In recent times they have been introduced into Alaska, USSR, Norway and elsewhere. They live exclusively in Arctic tundra where they feed on a variety of vegetation, particularly grasses, dwarf willow, sedges, moss and lichen. Herds of up to 100 can occur, but more usually they consist of 15-20 animals.

IBEX
Capra ibex

The **Ibex** or **Steinbok** is found in the Alps, the Himalayas, and the mountains of central Asia, Arabia and north Africa. They are very agile and live among rocky crags. At one time the only population in Europe was in the Gran Paradiso National Park, but populations have now been re-established in the Alps. The Ibex is closely related to the **Spanish Ibex** *C. pyrenaica*, which is found in the Iberian peninsula. The Ethiopian population, the **Walia** *C. ibex walia*, is regarded as a separate species.

BARBARY SHEEP *Ammotragus lervia*

The **Barbary Sheep** or **Aouadad** is now rare in the wild although they thrive in zoos and parks where several hundred are bred each year. Wild Barbary Sheep live in arid, rocky country with low vegetation where they hide from predators by remaining motionless. They also sand-bath which may help dust their hair to the same color as their habitat. They feed mostly in the morning or early evening on grass, the leaves of bushes and other desert vegetation, and rely on dew for moisture.

MOUNTAIN GOAT *Oreamnos americanus*

The **Mountain Goat** once ranged across the mountainous regions of North America from southeastern Alaska through Canada, to Oregon and Montana. It is not a true goat, but related to the Chamois. Since the 1920s, they have been reintroduced into areas from which they had originally been exterminated, and also into new areas, such as Oregon, Nevada, Utah, Colorado, Wyoming and South Dakota. Mountain Goats are up to 6½ ft. long, plus a short tail of up to 8 in., and can weigh up to 250 lbs., but average 185 lbs. The males are up to a third larger than females, and carry larger horns; an average horn length is 9 in., but they can be up to 1 ft. They inhabit very rugged inaccessible parts of the mountains, often perched on ledges or in the alpine meadows, feeding on grasses, sedges and succulent herbs. They are preyed on by pumas, eagles, brown bears, wolves and coyotes, particularly when young. The rutting season is in late autumn. When courting a female (nannie), the male (billy) approaches her and gives her a quick kick in the side! The males rarely actually fight, but when they do, their short horns can inflict serious wounds. The young – usually a single kid, but twins are not rare and triplets occur occasionally – are born after a gestation of about 178 days, in late spring or early summer. The kids follow their mother very closely and are weaned by late summer, but still stay with her until the next spring. Both sexes mature at about 2-3 years; in the wild they have been known to live for up to 18 years.

WILDEBEEST

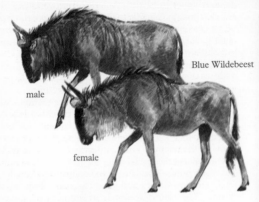

Blue Wildebeest

male

female

Black Wildebeest

There are 2 species of wildebeest or gnu. The **Blue Wildebeest** or **Brindled Gnu** *Connochaetes taurinus* is found in open grassland, plains and savannahs in eastern and southern Africa. Within historic times its range was much greater, but it has been exterminated in many areas. The Blue Wildebeest grows to a length of up to 8 ft., stands up to 5 ft. at the shoulder, has a tail of up to 3 ft. and weighs up to 640 lbs.; males are slightly larger than females and have horns up to 2 ft. 9 in. long.

The **Black Wildebeest** *C. gnou* was once widespread in the veldt and plains of southern Africa, but exterminated in the wild during the nineteenth century. Fortunately, small populations were saved on private farms, government reserves and zoos. The Black Wildebeest is slightly smaller than the Blue. Gnus are an important prey for many carnivores, including lion, leopard and hyena; scavengers will feed on the remains of kills. They also suffer from outbreaks of rinderpest, and, when migrating, large numbers often drown while crossing rivers, or get trampled to death. A single calf is born after a gestation of about 8 months; within a particular herd most of the births usually occur within short periods of 2-3 weeks and females defend the young against jackals and hyenas. Within a few minutes of birth the calf is able to follow the mother. Gnus become independent at about 1 year old and the males are driven away and join bachelor herds. In the wild, they have lived for 18 years, and in captivity for over 21 years.

PANGOLINS

Cape Pangolin

Pangolins, or scaly anteaters, are confined to the Old World, with 3 species found in southern Asia and 4 in Africa. The largest species, the **Giant Ground Pangolin** *Manis gigantea,* is found in Africa in savannah country from Senegal and Uganda south to Angola. It grows to a total length of nearly 6 ft. and weighs up to 77 lbs. The Cape or **Temminck's Ground Pangolin** *M. temmincki* is also found in open bush country, from the Sudan and East Africa to Botswana, Namibia and South Africa (except the southern Cape). The upper body is covered with overlapping scales resembling those of a reptile, but, like rhino horn, made of compressed hair.

There are two species of tree pangolin in Africa, the **Long-tailed** or **Black-bellied** *Manis tetradactyla* and the **White-bellied** *M. tricuspis* (illustrated). Both species are found in rainforests from Senegal, west to north-east Zaire and Uganda and south to Angola. The Black-bellied Pangolin grows to a length of 16 in., plus a tail of up to 2½ ft. and weighs up to 7 lbs.; the White-bellied Pangolin is slightly smaller, with a shorter tail. Both species are nocturnal, hiding in tree holes by day and are excellent climbers. On the underside of the tail they have a naked area which is used as a prehensile grip when climbing. They feed on ants and termites, which they extract from under bark and in fungi etc. with their long extendable tongue. The White-bellied Pangolin gives birth to a single young which stays in the nest hole for the first week and is then carried on the mother's tail. They start to eat insects at about 2 weeks and are independent at about 4-5 months and driven away at about 7-8 months. In captivity, they have lived for 3 years, but the **Indian Pangolin** *M. crassicaudata* has lived for over 13 years. The Asian Pangolins are extensively hunted because of the alleged medicinal value of their scales, which are used in the Far East to treat skin diseases.

SQUIRRELS

Indian Palm Squirrel

Red Squirrel

The **Red Squirrel** *Sciurus vulgaris* is widespread across the Old World from Ireland to Hokkaido in the Far East. It is found in coniferous and mixed forests. It grows to a length of up to 10 in., plus a tail of up to 8 in. and in Britain its tail and ear tufts gradually bleach until, just before they moult in the early summer, they are nearly white. In the British Isles, its populations have fluctuated widely; it became extinct in Ireland, but was subsequently reintroduced. In England, it is now all but extinct and has been replaced by the Grey Squirrel. In North America, 2 species of Red Squirrel occur: the **Eastern** or **American Red Squirrel** *Tamiasciurus hudsonicus* and **Douglas's Squirrel** *T. douglasi*.

The **American Gray Squirrel** *Sciurus carolinensis* is widespread in south-eastern Canada and eastern USA and has been introduced in several of the western states, and into Britain. It is now commonly found over most of England and Wales, as well as parts of Scotland.

There are 2 species of Giant Forest Squirrel, the **Slender-tailed Giant Forest Squirrel** *Protoxerus aubinni* found in West Africa from Liberia to Ghana; and the Oil-palm Squirrel *P. stangeri* which ranges from Sierra Leone to Kenya and Angola. The **Indian** or **Three-striped Palm Squirrel** *Funambulus palmarum* is one of the 5 species of Palm or Striped Squirrel found in the Indian subcontinent and Sri Lanka. Its repetitive shrill, birdlike call is a distinctive sound in forests.

PRAIRIE DOGS AND MARMOTS

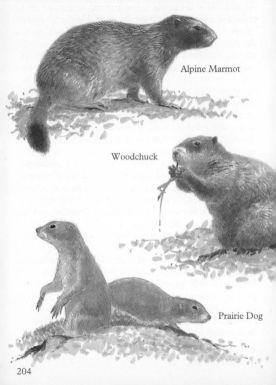

Alpine Marmot

Woodchuck

Prairie Dog

There are 11 species of marmot, found in the more temperate parts of the northern hemisphere. One of the best known species in the Old World is the **Alpine Marmot** *Marmota marmota* which is found above the treeline in the Alps and the Carpathians and has been introduced into the Pyrenees. It grows to a length of 2 ft. 4 in., plus a tail of 6 in., and weighs up to 17 lbs. It lives in colonies and emerges from the burrows as the sun strikes the mountain side to sunbathe before feeding. During the winter months it hibernates.

The **Woodchuck** *M. monax* is found in the north-eastern states of the USA, much of Canada and southeastern Alaska. It is smaller than the Alpine Marmot, and lives in open wooded habitats. There are several other related species in North America including the rare **Vancouver Island Marmot** *M. vancouverensis*, and the **Olympic Marmot** *M. olympus*, confined to the Alpine zone of the Olympic mountains in Washington. The Vancouver Island Marmot is reduced to less than 150 individuals in four separate areas; although protected under British Columbia law, they are threatened by logging and ski development.

Prairie dogs are ground-dwelling squirrels superficially similar to the marmots. The most widespread is the **Black-tailed Prairie Dog** *Cynomys ludovicianus*, which grows to a length of 1 ft., plus a tail of 4 in. and weighs up to 3 lbs. It lives in colonies, known as "towns", and because of its burrowing and crop raiding activities has been exterminated over much of its range.

Siberian Flying Squirrel

FLYING SQUIRRELS

Despite their name, flying squirrels are not capable of true flight – they can merely glide, using a membrane which stretches between the fore and hind limbs, and in some species between the hind limbs and tail. Most of the 35 species are found in Asia, and in particular the forests of Indo-China and South-east Asia. The largest of these are the **Giant Flying Squirrels** *Petaurista* spp. which grow to over 20 in. long, plus a tail of up to 2 ft., and weigh up to 5½ lbs. Outside eastern southern Asia, only 3 species are found, of which the **Siberian Flying Squirrel** *Pteromys volans* is one. This species occurs right across the northern mature forests of the Old World from Finland to Hokkaido. The two North American flying squirrels (*Glaucomys* spp.) are similar in appearance.

CHIPMUNKS

There are about 21 species of chipmunk, all of which are found in North America, except for the **Siberian Chipmunk** *Tamias sibiricus*. The most widespread and common species in eastern USA and Canada is the Eastern Chipmunk *T. striatus*, which is slightly larger than most other chipmunks, growing to a length of up to 7 in., plus a tail of up to 4 in. and weighing up to 5 oz. They are found in deciduous forests and more open areas with bushes and ground cover, living in burrows, in tunnels under logs, or among rock crevices. During the winter months they often hibernate. They eat a wide variety of vegetable matter including fungi, fruit and berries and will also eat insects, birds' eggs and small mammals. They have large cheek pouches on either side of the head in which they store food.

Eastern Chipmunk

SMALL RODENTS

Pocket Gopher

Spiny Mouse

Gerbil

Rodents are the most numerous group of mammals in the world, with the greatest number of species and probably the greatest number of individuals. Although there are over 1,600 species of rodent, only a tiny handful of them are ever seen in zoos. The **Pocket Gopher** family (*Geomyidae)* comprises some 37 species found in North and Central America. They are burrowing animals, and their lips can be closed behind their front teeth so that they can use them to dig without getting mouthfuls of soil. Their name derives from the fur-lined pouches on the sides of the head used for carrying food.

The 5 species of spiny mice *Acomys* spp, occur in Africa and the Middle East. The most familiar is the **Cairo Spiny Mouse** *A. cahirinus* which is found across north Africa, through the Middle East to Pakistan, and also on the island of Crete. They are very adaptable and live on dry seeds and grasses, and have also been reported eating the dried flesh of mummies in Egyptian tombs.

There are over 70 species of gerbil and jird, which are found in the steppes and arid regions of Africa, and in central and western Asia. Most species are relatively easy to keep in captivity and breed freely, and a large number have been kept in laboratories, and a few are kept in larger zoos. The most frequently seen is the **Mongolian,** or **Clawed Jird** *Meriones unguiculatus,* which is the species most frequently sold in pet shops under the name "Gerbil". There is a serious risk, both in North America and parts of Europe, that if pets were to escape they could become serious pests.

BEAVERS

Canadian Beaver

There are 2 species of beaver; the **American Beaver** *Castor canadensis,* which was once widespread over North America as far as northern Mexico, and the Eurasian Beaver *C. fiber*, which was once found over most of Europe, except the southern peninsulas, and east through Russia to the Altai. Although now extinct over most of Europe, there have been successful reintroduction programs and they are found in many parks and reserves. They are among the world's largest rodents, growing to 2 ft. 7 in., plus a broad, paddle-like tail of up to 18 in., and weighing up to 55 lbs., occasionally 88 lbs. The preferred habitat is well-wooded, slow flowing rivers and marshes with bushes and undergrowth. They build dams, dig canals and tunnels and construct lodges, depending on the habitat, in order to regulate the water level and transport logs. They normally fell fairly small trees, but have been known to fell trees up to 3 ft. in diameter. Beavers usually pair for life and mate in January or February. The young are born between April and June. There are 2-4 young in a litter, which become independent when they are nearly 2. In the wild, they are believed to have lived for at least 21 years. Beavers have been extensively hunted for their fur, which was "felted" for high quality hats, and for the *castoreum* from their scent glands. In early Christian Europe, they were eaten during fasts as fish on account of their scaly tails. The American Beaver was one of the mainstays of the economy during the early colonial explorations of New England and Canada and was hunted to extinction in many areas. They are still important to the fur trade but unlike other fur-bearing species, are not normally farmed or ranched. In recent years, they have been reintroduced into many parts of the USA.

RATS

There are around 80 species of true rat *Rattus* in the world, but possibly more await discovery. They include the Black or Ship Rat *Rattus rattus* which has spread to most parts of the world associated with humans; the **Brown** or **Norway Rat** *R. norvegicus* which is also a human associate and found almost worldwide; and the **Polynesian Rat** *R. exulans* from Burma and Indo-China which humans have spread all over the Pacific. Many species of rat cause considerable damage to agricultural produce and other property and are responsible for the spread of epidemic diseases such as Bubonic Plague. There are many species of rat confined to small areas, particularly in the Far East, and some of these may become rare as forests are destroyed.

DORMICE

Fat Dormouse

Hazel Dormouse

The 14 species are confined to the Old World. The most familiar is the **Hazel or Common Dormouse** *Muscardinus avellanarius* of Europe and Asia Minor, which falls asleep at the Mad Hatter's tea party in *Alice in Wonderland*. The name is derived from *dorm*, meaning sleep. It is found in deciduous woodlands and prefer hazels and honeysuckle.

PORCUPINES

Indian
Crested
Porcupine

North American
Porcupine

There are 2 families of porcupine: the 12 species of Old World porcupine and the 9 species of New World porcupine. New World porcupines are mainly arboreal; while Old World species are mostly terrestrial, burrowing rodents. The Old World porcupines are found throughout Africa and southern Asia, and the **Crested Porcupine** *Hystrix cristata* occurs in parts of Europe; it is also widespread in Africa as far south as Tanzania and Zaire. The other species of Old World porcupine commonly seen in zoos is the **Indian Crested Porcupine** *H. indica* which is found throughout the drier parts of the Indian sub-continent. The long quills on the back can be erected into a crest, but contrary to popular belief they cannot be propelled at attackers. They are merely rather loosely attached at the base, so that if they become embedded in an attacker they detach themselves. Septic wounds from porcupine quills embedded in tigers' paws can be the cause of tigers becoming man-eaters.

The **North American Porcupine** *Erithizon dorsatum* is found from northern Alaska, across northern Canada and the northeast USA and the western States as far south as northern Mexico. It grows to a length of up to 3 ft., plus a tail of up to 1 ft., and weighs up to 15 lbs. — occasionally much more. The preferred habitat is mixed woodland and forest, but it lives in a wide variety of other habitats from tundra to desert. A single young (occasionally twins) is born after a gestation of up to 217 days and is active soon after birth, reaching maturity at about 2 years, and has lived for over 10 years.

MARA *Dolichotis patagonum*

The **Mara** or **Patagonian Cavy** is a rodent which looks rather like a deer or hare, and lives in open arid areas of central and southern Argentina. It is greyish brown above and whitish below. Although related to the guinea pigs and cavies, they have evolved a body shape more like a deer, and on the hind feet, 3 toes have rather hoof-like claws. The forefeet have 4 toes with sharp claws which are used for excavating their burrows. They are extremely fast, and have been timed to run for over half a mile at 30 mph. Maras are largely diurnal and feed on a wide range of vegetation.

CAPYBARA *Hydrochoeris hydrochaeris*

The **Capybara** is the largest living rodent, growing to a length of 4 ft., standing up to 20 in. at the shoulder and weighing over 110 lbs. It is found from Panama south, east to the Andes, to Uruguay and northern Argentina. They are semi-aquatic, living in densely vegetated areas close to rivers, lakes and marshes, swimming with only the nostrils, eyes and ears above the surface, rather like hippos in Africa. They normally feed on land in the early morning and in the evening mainly on grasses, but also on aquatic plants and melons, squashes, and other crops. Although still widespread, they have undergone drastic declines in many areas mainly because they are hunted for their meat and hides; the fat is also used in medicine. Where they have been persecuted, they tend to be nocturnal.

CHINCHILLAS

Long-tailed Chinchilla

There are 2 very closely related chinchillas: the **Long-tailed Chinchilla** *Chinchilla laniger* and the **Short-tailed Chinchilla** *C. brevicaudata*. They grow to about 15 in. plus a tail of up to 6 in., and weigh up to 30 oz; the females are larger than the males. The fashion for making clothing from chinchilla fur goes back at least to the Incas. Their fur is now among the most valuable in the world, and this is because it is incredibly fine, soft and dense, with up to 60 hairs growing from each follicle. Chinchillas live high in the Andes at altitudes of 10,000-16,500 ft., the Short-tailed Chinchilla was once found at higher altitudes in Peru, Bolivia, Chile and possibly Argentina, but is now confined to Chile. The Long-tailed Chinchilla is confined to one small area in Chile. Their decline is almost entirely as a result of over-hunting for the fur trade – in the 1900s over 500,000 Chinchilla pelts were exported from Chile each year. Since the 1920s, the Long-tailed Chinchilla has been bred in fur farms in very large numbers, and it is this species which is commonly seen in zoos; however, the Short-tailed Chinchilla is the more valuable species. Chinchillas live in barren, rocky areas in rock clefts and burrows, emerging in the evening to feed on leaves, seeds and fruits; occasionally they have been seen to sun-bathe. They usually produce 2 litters a year, of up to 6 young, after a gestation of about 111 days. The young are weaned at 6-8 weeks and mature at about 8 months. In captivity, they have lived for over 20 years.

Chinchilla sunbathing in the early morning sun

COYPU *Myocastor coypus*

The **Coypu** is a large rodent, growing up to a length of over 2 ft., plus a tail of 16 in., and weighing up to 22 lbs., occasionally more. Looking like large rats, they are usually the animals displayed as giant sewer rats in circuses and street fairs. Originally found in aquatic habitats in South America from Chile and Argentina to southern Brazil and Bolivia, the Coypu has been extensively introduced into other parts of the world on fur farms. Some of these have escaped and Coypu now live in Europe, central Asia, Japan, Canada and the USA. In the 1920s, many fur farms were started for their valuable fur (known as Nutria to furriers). However, the market collapsed and they were either released or escaped from poorly built pens. Coypu have subsequently become serious pests in some of the areas they have colonised. In Louisiana, Coypu trapping has become an important industry and by the 1950s it was estimated that there were 20 million in the wild and in one year nearly 2 million were trapped. In their native South America, they are also utilized for food and occasional attempts have been made to popularize it in Britain. It is apparently illegal to sell it for human consumption in the USA. Coypu are prolific breeders, producing 2 litters a year of 2-9 (usually up to 5) young after a gestation of 130 days. The young are fully-furred and active, and can be independent a week after birth, but usually remain with the mother for 6-10 weeks, and are sexually mature at 3-7 months. Coypu have lived for over 6 years in captivity.

Coypu burrows
in riverbank

COMMON RABBIT *Orytolagus cuniculus*

The **Common Rabbit** is the ancestor of all the domesticated breeds of rabbit. They have spread, or been introduced, into most parts of the world and as a single doe can produce over 30 young a year, their populations soon escalate. In order to reduce the number of rabbits, the viral disease *Myxomatosis* was introduced into many areas including England, France and Australia. Rabbits are mainly grazers, feeding on grasses and other flowering plants, but they also eat bark and shoots, particularly in hard weather, and can cause considerable damage to crops such as winter wheat. They are preyed on by a wide range of animals including stoats, foxes, and buzzards.

American Pika

PIKAS

There are about 14 species of **Pika** *Ochotona* spp., occuring over most of northern Asia, as well as North America and Canada. They grow to about 8 in. long, and have no external tail and weigh around 7 oz. Pikas have 5 well separated fingers and toes and are quite unlike rabbits and hares; however, their teeth are very similar. Active by day, they make haystacks in preparation for the winter, gathering grasses and other plants and leaving them to dry in the sun, and in winter they remain active, tunnelling beneath the snow and feeding on their supply of hay. In summer they also forage for roots and grass and their bleating call can be heard as they scamper away among rocks.

HARES

Brown Hare

Hares are widespread, found throughout the northern hemisphere and Africa. They have also been introduced into South America, Australia and New Zealand. One of the most widespread is the **Brown Hare** *Lepus capensis* which occurs in Europe, northern Asia and over most of Africa. They live in a wide variety of habitats, but prefer open, deciduous woodlands and cultivated lands. Brown Hare populations are known to fluctuate: in the 1990s, a virus known as European Brown Hare Syndrome appears to be causing declines in some populations. The **Arctic Hare** *L. timidus* is found in the colder regions of Europe, Asia and North America and also in the Alps. The Arctic Hare is white in winter, but molts into grey-brown pelage in summer.

SUMATRAN RABBIT Nesolagus netscheri

The **Sumatran** (or **Short-eared**) **Rabbit** is thought to be one of the world's rarest mammals. Very little is known about its present distribution and status but they appear to be confined to the Barisan range of mountains in S.W. Sumatra. Found in forested areas, they are suffering from loss of habitat through forest clearance. Mostly nocturnal, they hide in burrows by day and are rarely encountered by humans: a possible sighting in 1978 is the only record after 1916. The **Bushman** (or **Riverine**) **Rabbit** *B. monticularis*, which occurs in small numbers in South Africa, is also considered to be critically endangered. Unlike the Sumatran Rabbit, it has particularly long ears and is rather hare-like. Other endangered rabbits include the **Amami Rabbit** *Pentalagus furnessi*, found only in islands south of Japan, and the **Volcano Rabbit** *Romeralgus diazi* and the **Omilteme Rabbit** *Sylvilagus insonus*, both of which only occur in Mexico.

Sumatran Rabbit

ELEPHANT SHREWS

Checkered Elephant Shrew

The 15 species of elephant shrew are found over most of Africa, except for the west, in a variety of habitats ranging from semi-desert to forests. Although they are insectivorous and shrew-like in many ways, they are often thought to be most closely related to rabbits and rodents; they vary from rat- to mouse-sized.

The **Rufous Elephant Shrew** *Elephantulus rufescens* grows to 6 in., plus a tail of 6½ in., and weighs up to 2 oz. It occurs in the savannah country of East Africa from Somalia to Tanzania. Like most elephant shrews, it is primarily diurnal and ground-living. It lives in pairs in burrows among rocks, in termite mounds and tree roots. When foraging, they walk slowly on all four limbs, but when alarmed, hop on their hind limbs with a very bouncy gait. One young (occasionally 2) is born after a gestation of 50 days; it is active from birth and independent at 2 months, with a life span of up to 3 years. Elephant shrews are preyed on by many small carnivores, birds of prey, and snakes.

Rufous Elephant Shrew

INDEX OF COMMON NAMES

Aardvark, 152
Alpaca, 164
Anteater, Dwarf, 20
Anteater, Giant, 20
Anteater, Spiny, 8
Antelope, Four-horned, 189
Aouadad, 195
Ape, Black, 62
Armadillo, Fairy, 24
Armadillo, Giant, 24
Armadillo, Nine-banded, 24
Ass, African Wild, 140
Ass, Asiatic Wild, 140
Aye-aye, 48

Baboon, Chacma, 64
Baboon, Guinea, 64
Baboon, Hamadryas, 64
Baboon, Olive, 64
Baboon, Yellow, 64
Badger, American, 90
Badger, Eurasian, 90
Bat, Common
   Long-eared, 44

Bat, Egyptian Fruit, 40
Bat, Greater Horseshoe, 46
Bat, Greater Indian Fruit, 40
Bat, Grey Long-eared, 44
Bat, Long-eared, 44
Bat, Vampire, 43
Bear, Grizzly, 81
Bear, Koala, 17
Bear, Polar, 82
Bear, Spectacled, 80
Bear, Brown, 81
Beaver, American, 210
Beaver, Eurasian, 210
Bison, American, 186
Bison, European, 186
Blackbuck, 189
Boar, Wild, 154
Bobcat, 104
Bongo, 182
Bonobo, 74
Buffalo, Asiatic Water, 184
Burro, 140
Bushbaby, Senegal, 50

Cachalot, 131
Camel, Arabian, 162
Camel, Bactrian, 162
Capybara, 217
Caracal, 104

Caribou, 172
Cat, Native, 19
Cavy, Patagonian, or Mara, 216
Chamois, 192
Cheetah, 114
Chimpanzee, 74
Chimpanzee, Pygmy, 74
Chinchilla, Long-tailed, 218
Chinchilla, Short-tailed, 218
Chipmunk, 207
Chipmunk, Eastern, 207
Chipmunk, Siberian, 207
Chowsingha, 189
Colobus, Angolan Black and White, 68
Colobus, Black, 68
Colobus, Olive, 68
Colobus, Red, 68
Colugo, 38
Cougar, 106
Cougar, Mountain Lion or Puma, 106
Coypu, 220

Dassie, Cape, 150
Deer, Black-tailed, 174
Deer, Mule, 174
Deer, Père David's, 168

Deer, Red, or Wapity, 166
Deer, White-tailed, 174
Desman, Pyrennean, 34
Dolphin, Bottle-nosed, 124
Dolphin, Gill's Bottle-nosed, 124
Dormouse, Hazel or Common, 213
Douroucouli, 54
Dugong, 132
Dusky, or Spectacled Langur, 70

Echidna, Long-beaked, 8
Echidna, Short-nosed, 8
Eland, Common, 183
Eland, Giant, 183
Eland, Lord Derby's, 183
Elephant, African, 134
Elephant, Asiatic or Indian, 136
Elephant Shrew, Checkered, 226
Elephant Shrew, Rufous, 226
Elephant Shrew, Short-eared, 226
Elk, or Moose, 170
Ermine, 88

Ferret, Black-footed, 93
Flying Fox, Indian, 40
Flying Lemur, 3
Flying Phalanger, 18
Flying Squirrel, 18, 206
Flying Squirrel,
  Siberian, 206
Fox, Arctic, 77
Fox, Bengal, 78
Fox, Cape, 78
Fox, Flying, 40
Fox, Indian Flying, 40
Fox, North American, 78
Fox, Pale, 78
Fox, Red, 78
Fox, Sand, 78
Fruit Bat, Egyptian, 40
Fruit Bat,
  Greater Indian, 40

Galago, Allen's, 50
Galago, Demidoff's, 50
Galago, Greater
  or Thick-tailed, 50
Galago, Western
  Needle-clawed, 50
Gerbil, Mongolian, 208
Gibbon, Silvery, 72
Gibbon, Common, 72

Gibbon, Dark-handed, 72
Gibbon, Grey, 72
Gibbon, Lar, 72
Gibbon, White-handed, 72
Giraffe, 176
Gnu, Brindled, 198
Goat, Mountain, 196
Gopher, Pocket, 208
Gorilla, Mountain, 73
Guanaco, 164
Gueraza, 68

Hare, Arctic, 224
Hare, Brown, 224
Hedgehog, 28
Hippopotamus, 160
Hippopotamus,
  Pygmy, 160
Horse, Przewalski's, 138
Horse, Wild, 138
Hyena, Brown, 102
Hyena, Spotted, 102
Hyena, Striped, 102
Hyrax, Large-toothed
  Rock, 150
Hyrax, Tree, 150

Ibex, 194
Ibex, Spanish, 195

Ichneuman, 100
Indri, 48

Jaguar, 112
Jird, Clawed, 208

Kangaroo, Grey, 12
Kangaroo, Tree, 12
Kiang, 140
Koala Bear, 17

Langur, Common, 70
Langur, Hanuman, 70
Lemur, Flying, 39
Lemur, Leaping, 48
Lemur, Mouse, 48
Lemur, Ring-tailed, 48
Leopard, 113
Linsang, African, 98
Linsang, Banded, 98
Lion, 108
Lynx, European, 104

Macaque, Bonnet, 62
Macaque, Celebes, 62
Macaque, Japanese, 63
Macaque, Rhesus, 62
Macaque, Toque, 62
Manatee, African, 132

Manatee, Amazon, 132
Manatee, American, 132
Mara, or Patagonian
  Cavy, 216
Marmoset,
  Long-tusked, 60
Marmoset, Pygmy, 60
Marmot, Alpine, 204
Marmot, Olympic, 204
Marmot, Vancouver
  Island, 204
Mink, European, 92
Mink, Wild American, 92
Moles, 32
Mole, Gunning's
  Golden, 35
Mole, Star-nosed, 33
Mongoose, Egyptian, 100
Mongoose, Indian
  Grey, 100
Monkey, Black Spider, 58
Monkey,   Black-handed
  Spider, 58
Monkey, Brown-headed, 58
Monkey, Common
  Squirrel, 56
Monkey, Grivet, 66
Monkey, Long-haired, 58
Monkey, Night, 54

Monkey, Owl, 54
Monkey, Red-backed, 56
Monkey, Savannah, 66
Monkey, Tantalus, 66
Moonrat, 28
Moose or Elk, 170
Mountain Lion, Cougar,
  or Puma, 106
Mouse, Spiny, 208

Ocelot, 107
Okapi, 178
Orang-utan, 75
Oryx, White or
  Arabian, 188
Otter, Eurasian, 96
Ox, Musk, 193

Panda, Giant, 86
Pangolin,
  Black-bellied, 200
Pangolin, Cape, 200
Pangolin, Giant
  Ground, 200
Pangolin, Indian, 200
Pangolin,
  Long-tailed, 200
Pangolin,
  Temminck's, 200

Pangolin,
  White-bellied, 200
Peccary, Chaco, 158
Peccary, Collared, 158
Peccary,
  White-lipped, 158
Phalanger, Flying, 18
Pika, 223
Platypus, Duck-billed, 9
Polecat, European, 93
Polecat, Marbled, 93
Polecat, Steppe, 93
Porcupine, Crested, 214
Porcupine, Indian
  Crested, 214
Porcupine, North
  American, 214
Possum, Brush-tailed, 10
Prairie Dog,
  Black-tailed, 204
Pronghorn, 180
Puma, Cougar or
  Mountain Lion, 106

Quagga, 139
Quoll, Eastern, 19

Rabbit, Amami, 225
Rabbit, Bushman

or Riverine, 225
Rabbit, Common, 222
Rabbit, Omilteme, 225
Rabbit, Sumatran
  or Short-eared, 225
Rabbit, Volcano, 225
Raccoon, 84
Racoon, Crab-eating, 84
Rat, Black, 212
Rat, Brown or
  Norway, 212
Rat, Polynesian, 212
Rat, Ships, 212
Reindeer, 172
Rhinoceros, Asian, 146
Rhinoceros, Black, 144
Rhinoceros, Indian, 146
Rhinoceros, Javan, 146
Rhinoceros, Sumatran or
  Hairy, 147
Rhinoceros, White or
  Square-Lipped, 142
Rorqual, Common, 128

Seal, Baikal, 123
Seal, Common, 122
Seal, Elephant, 120
Sea-lion, Californian, 116
Sheep, Barbary, 195

Shrew, Bicolored, 30
Shrew, Common, 30
Shrew, Elephant, 226
Shrew, Lesser
  White-toothed, 30
Shrew, Pygmy, 30
Shrew, Pygmy
  White-toothed, 30
Shrew, Rufous
  Elephant, 226
Shrew, Southern
  Water, 30
Sifaka, 49
Skunk, Hog-nosed, 94
Skunk, Hooded, 94
Skunk, Spotted, 94
Skunk, Striped, 94
Sloth, Three-toed, 22
Sloth, Two-toed, 22
Spectacled, or Dusky
  Langur, 70
Springbok, 190
Squirrel, American
  Gray, 203
Squirrel, American
  Red, 203
Squirrel, Douglas', 203
Squirrel, Flying, 18, 206
Squirrel, Oil-palm, 203

Squirrel, Red, 202
Squirrel, Siberian
    Flying, 206
Squirrel, Slender-tailed
    Giant Forest, 203
Squirrel, Three-striped
    Palm, 203
Squirrel Glider, 18
Steinbok, 194
Stoat, 88
Sugar Glider, 18

Tamandua, 20
Tamarin, Lion, 60
Tamarin, Red-handed, 60
Tamarin, White-lipped, 60
Tapir, Baird's, 148
Tapir, Brazilian, 148
Tapir, Malay, 148
Tapir, Mountain, 148
Tarsier, Horsfield's, 52
Tarsier, Philippine, 53
Tarsier, Sulawesi, 53
Tenrec, 26
Tiger, 110

Vervet, 66
Vicuna, 164

Walia, 195
Walrus, 118
Wapity, or Red Deer, 166
Warthog, 156
Weasel, 88
Whale, Blue, 128
Whale, Fin, 128
Whale, Humpback, 130
Whale, Killer, 126
Whale, Minke, 128
Whale, Sei, 128
Whale, Sperm, 131
Wildebeest, Black, 198
Wildebeest, Blue, 198
Wisent, 186
Wombat, 16
Woodchuck, 204

Yak, Wild, 185

Zebra, Common, 139
Zebra, Grevy's, 139
Zebra, Mountain, 139

INDEX OF SCIENTIFIC NAMES

Acinonyx jubatus, 114
Acomys cahirinus, 208
*Ailuropoda
    melanoleuca,* 86
Alces alces, 170
Alopex lagopus, 77
*Amblysomus
    gunningi,* 35
Ammotragus lervia, 195
*Antidorcas
    marsupialis,* 190
*Antilocapra
    americana,* 180
Antilope cervicapra, 189
Aotus trivirgatus, 54
Ateles belzebuth, 58
Ateles fusciceps, 58
Ateles geoffroyi, 58
Ateles paniscus, 58

Balaena acutorostrata, 128
Balaena borealis, 128
Balaena musculus, 128
Balaenoptera physalus, 128
Bison bison, 186

Bos grunniens, 185
Bradypus torquatus, 22
Bradypus tridactylus, 22
Bradypus variegatus, 22
Bubalis arnee, 184
Bubalis bubalis, 184
*Bunolagus
    monticularis,* 225

Callicebus spp., 54
Camelus dromedarius, 162
Camelus ferus, 162
Canis lupus, 76
Capra ibex, 194
Capra ibex walia, 195
Capra pyrenaica, 195
Castor canadensis, 210
Castor fiber, 210
Catagonus wagneri, 158
Cebuella pygmaea, 60
Ceratotherium simum, 142
Cercopithecus aethiops, 66
Cervus elaphus, 166
*Chinchilla
    brevicaudata,* 219
Chinchilla laniger, 219
*Chlamyphorus
    truncatus,* 24
Choeropsis liberiensis, 160

Choloepus hoffmanni, 22
Colobus badius, 68
Colobus polykomos, 68
Colobus satanus, 68
Condylura cristata, 33
Conepatus spp., 94
*Connochaetes
    taurinus,* 198
Coonochaetes gnou, 198
Crocidura, 30
Crocuta crocuta, 102
Cylopes didactylus, 20
Cynomys ludovicianus, 204

Dasogale fontoyonti, 26
*Dasypus
    novemcinctus,* 24
Dasyurus viverrinus, 19
*Daubentonia
    madagascariensis,* 48
Dendrohyrax spp., 150
Dendrolagus spp., 12
*Dicerorhinus
    sumatrensis,* 147
Diceros bicornis, 144
Dolichotis patagonum, 216

Echinops telfairi, 26
Echinosorex gymnurus, 28

*Elaphurus
    davidianus,* 168
*Elephantulus
    rufescens,* 226
Elephas maxima, 136
Equus africanus, 140
Equus asinus, 140
Equus burchelli, 139
Equus ferus, 138
*Equus ferus
    przewalskii,* 138
Equus grevyi, 139
Equus hemionus, 140
Equus kiang, 140
Equus quagga, 139
Equus zebra, 139
Erinaceus europaeus, 28
Erithizon dorsatum, 214
Euoticus egantulus, 50

Felis caracal, 104
Felis concolor, 106
Felis lynx, 104
Felis pardalis, 107
Felis rufus, 104
*Funambulus
    palmarum,* 203

Galago alleni, 50

Galago demifovi, 50
Galago senegalensis, 50
Galemys pyrenaica, 34
Giraffe camelopardalis, 176
Gorilla gorilla, 73

Hemiechinus auritus, 28
Herpestes edwardsi, 100
Herpestes ichneumon, 100
Hippopotamus amphibius, 160
Hyaena brunnea, 102
Hyaena hyaena, 102
Hydrochaeris hydrochaeris, 217
Hylobates lar, 72
Hystric cristata, 214
Hystrix indica, 214

Indri indri, 48

Lama glama, 164
Lama guanicoe, 164
Lama pacos, 164
Lasiorhinus latifrons, 16
Lemur catta, 48
Leontopithecus rosalia, 60
Lepus capensis, 224

Lepus timidus, 224
Limnogale mergulus, 26
Loxodonta african, 134
Lutra lutra, 96

Macaca fuscata, 63
Macaca mulatta, 62
Macaca nigra, 62
Macaca radiata, 63
Macaca sinica, 62
Macropus fuliginosus, 12
Macropus giganteus, 12
Manis crassicaudata, 200
Manis gigantea, 200
Manis temmincki, 200
Manis tetradactyla, 200
Manis tricuspis, 200
Marmota marmota, 204
Marmota monax, 204
Marmota olympus, 204
Marmota vancouverensis, 204
Megaptera novaeangliae, 130
Meles meles, 90
Mephitis macroura, 94
Mephitis mephitis, 94
Meriones unguiculatus, 208

*Muscardinus
  avellanarius,* 213
Mustela erminea, 88
Mustela eversmanni, 93
Mustela lutreola, 92
Mustela nigripes, 93
Mustela nivalis, 88
Mustela putorius, 93
Mustela vison, 92
Myocastor coypus, 220
*Myrmecophaga
  tridactyla,* 20

Neomys anomalus, 30
Nesolagus netscheri, 225

Odicoileus hemionus, 174
*Odicoileus
  virginianus,* 174
Odobenus rosmarus, 118
Okapia johnstoni, 178
Orcinus orca, 126
*Oreamnos
  americanus,* 196
*Ornithorhynchus
  anatinus,* 9
Orycteropus afer, 152
Orytolagus cuniculus, 222
Oryx leucoryx, 188

*Otolemur
  crassicaudatus,* 50
Otolemur garnetti, 50
Ovibos moschatus, 193

Pan paniscus, 74
Pan troglodytes, 74
Panthera leo, 108
Panthera onca, 112
Panthera pardus, 113
Panthera tigris, 110
Papio anubis, 64
Papio cynocephalus, 64
Papio hamadryas, 64
Papio papio, 64
Papio ursinus, 64
Pentalagus furnessi, 225
Petaurista, 206
Petaurista norfolkensis, 18
Petaurus breviceps, 18
*Phacochoerus
  aethiopicus,* 156
*Phascalarctos
  cinereus,* 17
Phoca sibirica, 123
Phoca vitulina, 122
Physeter catodon, 131
Plecotus auritus, 44
Plecotus austriacus, 44

Plecotus townsendi, 44
Poiana linsang, 98
Poiana richardsoni, 98
Pongo pygmaeus, 75
Presbytis entellus, 70
Presbytis obscura, 70
Priodontes maximus, 24
Procavia capensis, 150
Procolobus verus, 68
Procyon cancrivorus, 84
Procyon lotor, 84
Protoxerus aubinni, 203
Protoxerus stangeri, 203
Pteromys volans, 206
Pteropus giganteus, 40

Rangifer tarundus, 172
Rattus exulans, 212
Rattus norvegicus, 212
Rattus rattus, 212
*Rhinoceros
  sondaicus,* 147
*Rhinoceros
  unicornis,* 146
*Rhinolophus
  ferrumequinum,* 46
Romeralgus diazi, 225
Rousettus aegyptiacus, 40
Rupicapra rupicapra, 192

*Rupicapra rupicapra
  ornata,* 192

Saguinus labiatus, 60
Saguinus midas, 60
Saimiri oestedi, 56
Saimiri sciurus, 56
Sciurus carolinensis, 203
Sciurus vulgaris, 202
Setifer setosus, 26
Sorex araneus, 30
Sorex minutus, 30
Spilogale spp, 94
Sus scrofa, 154
Sylvilagus inconus, 225

Tachyglossus aculeatus, 8
Talpa europeae, 33
Tamandua mexicana, 20
*Tamandua
  tetradactyla,* 20
Tamias sibiricus, 207
Tamias striatus, 207
*Tamiasciurus
  douglasi,* 203
*Tamiasciurus
  hudsonicus,* 203
Tapirus bairdi, 148
Tapirus indicus, 148

Tapirus roulini, 148
Tapirus terrestris, 148
Tarsius bancanus, 52
Tarsius spectrum, 53
Tarsius syrichta, 53
Taxidea taxus, 90
Tayassu pecari, 158
Tayassu tajacu, 158
Tenrec ecaudatus, 26
*Tetracerus
   quadricornis*, 189
Thalarctos maritimus, 82
*Tragelaphus
   derbianus*, 183
*Tragelaphus
   euryceros*, 182
Tragelaphus oryx, 183
Tremarctos ornatus, 80
Trichechus inunguis, 132
Trichechus manatus, 132
*Trichechus
   senegelensis*, 132
*Trichosurus
   vulpecula*, 10
Tupaia glis, 36
Tursiops gilli, 124
Tursiops truncatus, 124

Ursus arctos, 81

Vicugna vicugna, 164
Vombatus ursinus, 16
Vormela peregusna, 93
Vulpes bengalensis, 78
Vulpes chama, 78
Vulpes fulva, 78
Vulpes pallida, 78
Vulpes rueppelli, 78
Vulpes vulpes, 78

Zaglossus brunijni, 8
*Zalophus
   californianus*, 116